The Authentic Child

ALAN DeWITT BUTTON

The Authentic
Child

RANDOM HOUSE

NEW YORK

FIRST PRINTING

9 8 7 6 5 4 3 2

Copyright © 1969 by Alan DeWitt Button

Library of Congress Catalog Card Number: 68–28564

Manufactured in the United States of America by The Book Press, Brattleboro, Vt.

Quotations on pp. 94, 169–70 from *Challenges of Humanistic Psychology*, by J. F. Bugental. Copyright 1967 by McGraw-Hill, Inc. Used by permission of McGraw-Hill Book Company.

Quotations on pp. 19, 40, 43, 51 from *Irrational Man*, by William Barrett. Copyright 1958 by William Barrett. Reprinted by permission of Doubleday & Company, Inc.

Quotation on p. 34 from *Identity: Youth and Crisis*, by Erik H. Erikson. Copyright 1968 by W. W. Norton & Company, Inc. Reprinted by permission of W. W. Norton & Company, Inc.

Quotation on p. 74 from "Misgiving" in *Complete Poems of Robert Frost*. Copyright 1923 by Holt, Rinehart and Winston, Inc. Copyright 1951 by Robert Frost. Reprinted by permission of Holt, Rinehart and Winston, Inc.

Quotation on pp. 32–33 from "Personality Organization in Children," by J. E. Anderson, from *The American Psychologist*, 1948, III, 409–416.

Quotation on p. 61 from *Collected Poems*, Harper and Row. Copyright 1923, 1951 by Edna St. Vincent Millay and Norma Millay Ellis.

An excerpt on pp. 126–27 from "What Do We Know About Learning" by Dr. Goodwin Watson is reprinted by permission from the *National Education Association Journal*, March, 1963.

Typography and binding design by Mary M. Ahern

Foreword

Three years ago, when our daughter Sara was seven, my wife left the house immediately after dinner one night to meet a friend at the airport. The friend's plane was due to arrive at seven, but by nine o'clock my wife had not returned. I had had a pleasant evening with Sara and the other children and had then put them to bed. Passing Sara's room after putting the baby down, I heard her quietly crying. I went in and asked her what the matter was. "I'm worried about Mommy," she sobbed. "She said she'd be right back, and it's been over two hours."

At first, automatically, I went through the routine reassurances that—because they are responses only to the content of what the child says—not only do not reassure but often make things worse. "Now don't worry, dear. Mother's all right . . . she would have called if there'd been any trouble . . . the plane was probably late."

As I should have known, these were empty statements, no matter how reasonable or, as it happened, correct they were. Sara, unreassured, continued to sob. I then realized that I was doing with my daughter what I would never do with my patients: I was patronizing her; I was denying her genuine feelings after she had trusted me enough to tell them to me; and I was using her to solve my own problems (for I was beginning to worry, too). Children have enough problems of their own without being saddled with those of their parents, I realized for approximately the eighty millionth time, and it seemed a very good idea to face the real issues.

I sat down on the bed and said, "I know how you feel, baby. It's an awful feeling when we're worried about someone we love. But it's especially hard for you, I think. I'm sure the plane was late, or something, so I'm just a *little* bit worried. But you're a child, and children have big worries. The thing you're worried about—that Mama maybe had an accident or something—is one of these big worries. All children have them, all the time, and they're rough. Maybe it's the roughest part of being a child, having these awful worries about someone you love and need so much." I stopped at this point—no doubt a good thing, since, warmed to my subject, I should probably have stiffened the child with a discussion of contingency, that presence in her life of the real possibility of disaster. But Sara, with a brave and relieved smile, had dropped off to sleep.

I have seen this brave relief on the faces and heard it in the voices of many children, adolescents, and college students when I have talked with them about contingency; about the unavoidable presence of anxiety in their lives; and about the action they can take upon recognizing it. I have seen also, much more frequently, the refusal to face contingency and the consequent invalid protest, the self-destructive rebellion, the self-annihilating irresponsibility of such refusal.

It is to the clarification of the differences between the acceptance of and the refusal to accept contingency, between the courageous decisions that follow upon its acceptance and the neurotic conflicts that follow upon its denial, that this book is directed.

And it is to my daughter Sara, who started me out on an expanding, enriching, and workable adaptation of certain principles of existential psychology to issues of child psychology, that it is dedicated.

Contents

Note to the Reader

The Authentic Child is not a "How to do it" manual for raising children. Indeed, the book is a plea for the abandonment of the "how to" approach, with its technical, specific guidelines for conduct which simply do not work in the complex interplay of parents and their children.

As is stated in Chapter XIV, "If we are to be authentic persons, and if our children are to be authentic, we must abandon, cast aside, transcend our need to be told what to do and how to do it!" Real help, I am convinced, is that which gives parents confidence in their own humanism, their own abilities to affect their children's lives meaningfully and positively. Telling them specifically what to do, on the other hand, can only hurt them by denying their own good sense as well as their humanism.

The reader is therefore duly warned that he will find an attitudinal, not a technical, viewpoint, and that he will search in vain for specific guidelines.

—A. D. B.

The Authentic Child

I:
The Statement

The Authentic Child is an attempt to translate certain
existential concepts into an understandable statement about children. "Freedom," "choice," "contingency," "anxiety," "despair," and their derivative concepts are existential terms which offer to child
psychology a fresh approach while adding to and
complementing its already substantial body of knowledge. They also offer to parents a fresh approach
which can expand and enrich the parent-child relationship and can help melt away past rigidities which
have turned the essential beauty of the relationship
into a nongrowing static mold of defeat. I have incorporated into the book concepts derived from the pattern of successes and failures I have experienced with
my child patients and their families in fifteen years of
experience as a clinical psychologist. These concepts,
"respect," "dignity," "autonomy," and "spontaneity,"
are also existential terms, for they are the terms of
living itself.

The most important concept in the book is love;

its discussion derives from existentialism, from academic and clinical psychology, from my own childhood and adulthood, and most of all from the immediate, concrete, and here-and-now experiences of my daily life. The levels of loving I reach in my contacts with family at home, students at the college where I teach, patients in my office, and friends and colleagues in between, give a richness and meaning to each day that I wish to share.

My experiences of success and failure with children, adolescents, college students, and adults have all been marked by intense emotional and intellectual involvement; and they have sometimes left me feeling triumphant or hopeful, and sometimes drained, dejected, or futile. These are the emotions that prompt me to write, just as it is emotion that prompts an adult to do anything meaningful to him and that prompts a child to exult or weep, to reach out or to strike out.

The challenge to the author, who must in the necessarily intellectual mode of writing try to communicate a raw and emotional, nonintellectual perception of children and their lives, is much like the challenge to parents, who must, if they are to be authentic parents, impose a template of reason upon the squirming, feeling, reacting child before them. The template, though rational and grounded as solidly as present knowledge allows in the experimental and theoretical findings of child psychology, is flexible and fragile.

4

If it is a rigid one of prohibitions, or expected, insisted-upon and closely regimented standards of behavior—if it is one that is based upon a point of view, perhaps ecclesiastical, that may have little or nothing to do with a child's real existence—if it is one based solely upon the parents' background and upbringing without reference to the changed styles and circumstances of the new generation's life—then it becomes suffocating, and the child's freedom to develop, together with his parents' freedom to develop with him as well as independently of him, are curtailed at best, permanently crippled at worst.

The template of reason must not be considered final or even authoritative. If it becomes rigidly applied its value disappears and it becomes a restricting straitjacket of artifice, rather than the adaptive mantle which, superimposed individually and lightly upon the unique emotional life of a child, provides the delicate but necessary rationality in the child's development. Existentialism, by its own terms, is evanescent and individual. It deals with the individual's life—not his brother's, or his mother's. If the tenets of existentialism are applied generally, indiscriminately, then they are no longer existential, and the result will be another harmful fraud which will increase the suffering of little children.

In the 1930's Watson's behavioristic psychology, with its inhuman insistence upon rigid schedules of child-rearing (an inhumanity still practiced by certain pediatricians in the 1960's) did its best to turn us into machines. It was slightly more successful with parents than with children, and these parents are the grandparents of today who make their daughters-in-law resent them and their admonitions about the dangers of simply loving their children and fulfilling their needs naturally and spontaneously.

When the pendulum had swung from rigidity to a movement of complete permissiveness—although never practiced as totally as its opponents would have us believe—children were once more harmed, this time by denying their need for structure, for firm models with whom to identify, for flexible standards of behavior against which they could test their own emerging behavior patterns, and for the clear communication of parental values and opinions in the face of which they could evolve their own.

Harm has also been done by the psychoanalytic movement, with its terrifying overstatements about the dread consequences of any deviations from a so-called "ideal" way of managing the many expressions of infantile and child sexuality. Mothers became reluctant to lie down with a frightened child for fear of infecting him with an irreversible Oedipus complex; fathers were afraid to quell or even to impose control upon a child's ungovernable temper tantrum because of the "sure" chance of repressing hostility and causing God knows what later on, from juvenile delinquency to high blood pressure. Such ludicrous inhibitions of natural parental reactions, even granting that many of the strictures are distortions of true psychoanalytic doctrine, have hampered the freedom of children's development, *and* that of their parents.

The current "operant conditioning" approach of B. F. Skinner in education, psychotherapy, and child-raising techniques has reported success with non-achieving, autistic, and delinquent youngsters. But the implications in its program of "positive and negative reinforcements" (rewards and punishments) and of the kind of rigid control of children, however appropriately such a program might shape behavior, cannot but stultify and further restrict the child's freedom of inner growth.

The operant conditioning technique is one in which the child—or the white rat, or the chimpanzee—"operates" on his environment by doing things such as pulling levers or pushing buttons that have previously been rewarded, or "reinforced," and, allegedly, *not* doing things that have previously been punished. Thus, autistic, mute children have been known to utter words following a sufficiently long and intense "reinforcement schedule." It is important to note that punishment, or "negative reinforcement," does *not*, in fact, eliminate undesirable behavior in the child or the rat or the chimp. There is apparently a strong need for symmetry on the part of psychologists of the operant persuasion, such that they continue to use punitive methods in their demonstrations and in

7

their therapies in a witless clinging to the idea that if rewards reinforce appropriate behavior, then punishment *must* eliminate negative behavior. The theory sounds wonderfully balanced, and it may please and confirm the philosophy of punitive parents (and psychologists), but it will not necessarily lead to the results desired.

It is certainly easier to live with and more convenient to have a conforming, achieving, well-programmed child. But he may grow into an automaton, afraid of creativity, unable to expand, maybe even unable to allow himself to experience the defenseless states of intimacy, of communion, of passion. He may, in short, be unable, or be incompletely able, to love. William Gibson's powerful drama *The Miracle Worker* shows vividly the advantages and disadvantages of the operant approach in training children. The blind, deaf, mute, animalistic little Helen Keller is trained, to be sure, into a conforming and docile little citizen by the reward-and-punishment schedule of her teacher. But she is not taught to think! The complex miracle of thinking can in no way be attributed to the training process. It is not possible to say how Helen began to think: her native intelligence, the disciplined affection she felt from and toward her teacher, her human quest for meaning and understanding—all play their parts. But the miracle of thought remains unexplained. It explodes from within, unaffected by outer proddings and pressures except as they may inhibit, but never promote; and it is nothing short of barbaric to assume that it can be controlled. Parents and governments may attempt thought control, but the real miracle of humanity is that the secure and confident individual, the one we want our child to be like, will forever resist; and the creative individual will not only rebel but will transcend the controls to reach new and original heights of thinking.

The anti-humanistic bias of the operant or "behavioristic" therapists is nowhere more clearly revealed than in their arbitrary decisions as to what is acceptable and what is unacceptable behavior for their charges; and what forms of behavior, therefore, should be rewarded and what should be punished. Their presumption is appalling; and their techniques, inhibitory of creative, innovative thinking, more so. They believe, it would seem, in absolute values. Yet values are functions of their times—witness the "generation gap"—relative to the times, to the individuals, and to the circumstances. It is comforting to many to believe that values are unchangeable. Many would like to believe, with the framers of the Constitution, that Blacks aren't really human—or, with lawmakers up to the time of women's suffrage, that women aren't either. We deny thought to children in the same way, with our controlling techniques. It is small wonder that they, like Blacks and women, finally rebel.

No parents, especially the many who sense their own deficiencies, will wish to inhibit their children in loving or in thinking. Yet the emphasis upon rewards and punishments inherent in the operant-conditioning approach, and its consequent prizing of overt behavior, can turn all behavior, including loving, into a simple matter of technique. Real love—intimacy, communion, and passion—is much more than a technique. It comes from within, it is spontaneous and unguarded, it is ungoverned, unregimented, and unscheduled. It cannot be programmed like the multiplication tables into a child's response repertoire, and attempts to do so will result in barren experience. The same applies to thinking, that exciting explosion of seeing connections and abstracting beyond them.

Why existentialism? Is this approach simply a new form of control, of rigidity, of destructiveness to a child's freedom of development? It can be, of course, and some future critic may well include it in the list of man's well-meaning but inadequate attempts to understand and to control the human condition. As it stands now, however—or as I understand it (there are as many existentialisms as there are existentialists, which offers both freedom and ambiguity to the would-be existentialist)—existentialism proclaims freedom, unfettered, often frightening freedom, and it is only in freedom that we can attain full humanity. There are no rules, no standards, no proscriptions or prescriptions in existentialism— no generalities, no lists of should and should nots to guide a human life. The absence of guidelines is irritating (and frightening) to the insecure parent. It is refreshing and meaningful and personally expanding to the secure parent who can now come right out and say, "I trust myself and my spontaneous reactions to my child, and I know that these cannot but be good for him."

Existentialism holds that authenticity—the condition of real-ness and full-functioning, of expanding sensitivity and awareness, of absorbed involvement in issues and work and people, of joy, and of love— is based upon a proud awareness of oneself as a living, choosing, self-determining, unique individual. The authentic person, further, grants authenticity to other persons, and his relations with them are grounded in a firm and mutual respect. It is this model that I have adopted as exemplary of the kind of parent-child relationship most conducive to the freedom of development of both child and parent and therefore most productive of healthy and secure persons.

Existentialism is a state of mind, an attitude, and a value system, and it is accordingly unmeasurable and unquantifiable. Its highest value is humanistic: the human experience, one's own and one's children's, is an experience of dignity and of respectful fascination, and it warrants thought and compassion. The authentic parent, one who values his child as worth-

while and important, has an authentic child. He likes
the child, loves him, respects him, and, so far as he
is able, understands him. He is interested in him
always, and more often than not, fascinated by him.
He remembers often, with pleasure, the events and
chronology of the child's past. He thinks at night, in
bed, of the child's future. But in the immediacy of
now, of today, of this minute, his emphasis is not
upon the past or future, but upon the child himself,
as he is at this moment.

The authentic parent wants *this* moment to be a
good one, both for the child and for himself. He says
something funny, or he puts his hand on the child's
head, or he smiles at the child, and it is a good
moment. It is not memorable, as moments of crisis or
violence or exuberance are apt to be. Yet it remains
with him, and with the child, quietly, for the rest
of the day. There is a solidity to it that strengthens
their two-ness for many days, and for life.

The authentic parent abhors anger. He senses the
delicacy, the fragility of his child's personality, and its
terrible vulnerability to anger. He has seen, despairingly, his child's face crumple under the onslaught
of shouts and abuse, of pain and fear. He has watched
the child's inadequate attempts to protect himself
against such violence—the lies, the closing off of
communication, the clear, unarticulated birth of resentment at injustice which can, and usually does,
develop into overt hatred and inevitable rebellion:

worse, into a core of violence central to the child himself that will, equally inevitably, explode against his own children in years to come.

What little anger there is in the authentic parent is rarely directed against his child. There is healthy anger against injustice, cruelty, bigotry, the senselessness of violence. There is some residual neurotic anger against people, stemming from the way he himself was brought up. He recognizes this, keeps much of it to himself, talks some of it over with his child, who thereby learns that anger is not to be denied but is to be controlled and can be controlled.

All this is a lengthy prelude to the simple statement: The authentic child is one who develops in freedom, thereby to become whole.

This Brave Relief

A sturdy, exhausted three-year-old stumbles doggedly after his father, his eyes and throat aching with his need to cry, his legs aching with his need to collapse. It's still another mile to the campsite, and his father has an armload of wood. There is nothing to do but to plod on, and he plods on, without tears and without complaints.

A sixteen-year-old girl, slender and lovely, protests her love for a nineteen-year-old unemployed school dropout, the very mention of whose name has kept her home in an ugly, screaming turmoil for more than a year. She has decided not to see the boy for two years, because she knows she is too young for marriage, and she has also decided not to tell her parents. "I haven't seen him for over a month already, and they still haven't caught on," she says. "It's funny, really. They're still yelling their heads off about nothing." She laughs with cold but genuine amusement. "They crack me up."

"I'm *not* afraid of the service, damn it," a college boy says defensively. "In fact," he says, grinning, "I'd sort of like to go. My brother says it's a blast—you know. But the point is, I've *got* to get my M.A. first. For plenty of good reasons. I'll be a lot more valuable to the service when I get it, for one thing. So I'm going to declare myself a CO. But I'm not a hypocrite. I'm not a killer, and I'm not going to be turned into one, either. Especially in this lousy war." He shrugs. "I've got my data already. If I go to prison, I can write the thing there." Another grin. "I'll call it *Mein Kampf.*"

The decision that brings relief, that keeps a child going, that brings self-respect, that allows the graceful touch of humor, that preserves and strengthens his identity, is a decision that takes courage to make. It is always made in adversity, if not in desperation. It is made under and against pressure—pressure from without and especially pressure from within.

It is not necessarily the best decision. One, least of all the decider, can't always know the best decision. But those who exert the external pressure know it even less. Other things being equal, a decision an adolescent makes which is contrary to the decision his parents wish him to make is, more often than not, a better one. But the decision which brings relief is probably the best decision, under the contemporary circumstances. It is a good decision not just because it brings self-respect and humor and a sense of identity, but because it does bring relief. And brave relief is a solution. It ends—often only temporarily, to be sure—the pain and anxiety of the cumulative pressures, rather than simply diverting and ultimately increasing them. For every brave decision there are hundreds of cowardly outs. There are tantrums and denials and blind revolts and lies and hypocrisies and violences—all ways of attenuating identity, of losing self-respect, of seeing oneself and one's world bleakly and humorlessly. Essentially, they don't work. They perpetuate despair and anxiety; they exacerbate inner and outer pressures. They are very costly.

The brave decision is better because it is made on the basis of personal responsibility. This is the conscious, though often inarticulate, thought that one really does know better than any parent, any government, any psychologist, any superhuman force just what *is* best for oneself-in-one's-circumstance.*

The stumbling child experiences his fatigue and his need to cry, and he simultaneously and inextricably experiences the "long way still to go," his father's expectations that he can do it, and his predictable disappointment were the child to choose the easy way and give in to his fatigue. He does not, incidentally, perceive—except, possibly, at some murky and forever unknowable level of

---

* The hyphens, awkward hallmarks of the existentialist writer, are unfortunately necessary to communicate the totality of the existential experience.

unconsciousness—past the exhortation "Be a man!" and the like. These may have had their influences (probably in the direction opposite to which they were intended), although it is doubtful. He knows now only that he is Johnny out for a hike to gather wood with his dad and it's better to plod on even if he feels like collapsing. He knows Daddy would put down the wood and carry him, all right, but the rewards of later praise from Dad are greater. Besides, he chose to go in the first place, even after Dad said it would be a long hike. A three-year-old, like everyone else, must maintain his self-respect. It is painful when he, and everyone else, does not.

Age three—or two, or even one—is not too young for such sophisticated "reasoning." It is not, of course, reasoning in the adult sense of the word. But it is problem-solving, and it is conflict-resolution. A less sturdy three-year-old may well give in to his fatigue and collapse in tears or tantrums. And he may well reap a harvest of scorn or disgust or name-calling from his father that will affect later conflict-resolutions to the point where he may predictably resolve them in the direction of tears and immobility ("laziness"). Yet many three-year-olds—and all of them, given the security of paternal helpfulness and love—are very well able to sense both sides of their conflict. They are the ones who carry on and who thereby reap the harvest of more praise from their fathers. They are the ones who, out of the desire to please and feeling the loving acknowledgment of this desire, carry on, to greater and greater degrees of endurance and achievement, all their lives.

Nietzsche, in *Also Sprach Zarathustra,* describes the validity of the personal decision in another way: "In the end, one experiences only oneself."

The cowardly decision is an evasion of this responsibility. It states that Mother, or the draft board, or the doctor, or God, knows better than I what I should do, or think, or be. The recognition that others with sympathy and experience sometimes really do know better than I is not, of course, a cowardly decision but simply a realistic evaluation of oneself as less experienced than others. It is a cowardly decision only when one's own powers of evaluation are totally denied in the overpowering presence of authority. Often, conversely, the cowardly decision states that mother, *et al.,* are pushing for precisely the wrong thing for me. In either case, whether submitting to or rebelling against the other's authority, one is in bondage to it at the same time that one remains irresponsible.

The willingness to assume personal responsibility is especially courageous when one considers the dearth of information young people are given about persons before them, and contemporaries with them, who have undertaken such responsibility in the face of strong social opposition—Thomas Jefferson, Ralph Waldo Emerson, Bertrand Russell, Cassius Clay,

Jesus Christ, Dr. Benjamin Spock, David Harris. The list, to humanity's endless glory, is long. The official media of society have made light of or overtly misrepresented these persons' stands; worse, they have labeled them eccentric, queer, draft dodger, hippie, Communist. That list, to humanity's endless disgrace, is long.

It is a brave thing to stand upon one's personal certitude against the prevailing climate. It is even braver to assume the derogatory label and its attendant self-doubting ("Maybe I am, after all, as they say, just a draft dodger"), for by this assumption, one questions the very thing his contrary stand is trying to assert and affirms that he is *not* one thing, that he is more than can be summed up in any single label, especially a derogatory one. William Barrett, in his powerful *Irrational Man,* states: ". . . a single impulse can be just as much an impulse toward love on the one hand as it is toward power on the other . . ."

A characteristic of the personally responsible person, the one who can make the brave decision, is his awareness of his complexity. He must deny being typed, whether for good or for ill, because he knows he is both. He "encompasses his polarities," as Everett Shostrom puts it, and it is on the basis of this complete and candid self-knowledge that he really does know better than anyone else just what is best for him. The pretty sixteen-year-old knows, whether she'll admit it to her parents or not, that she is far too young for marriage. She also knows she has the need and the passion to make a pretty good stab at it. It is her complete knowledge of herself that allows her to make the decision of a two-year postponement. It is most certainly not her parents' one-sided description of "immaturity." Indeed, she is fortunate that she has not allowed such a description to push her self-perception over to the equally one-sided conviction of readiness for marriage.

The little boy keeps struggling along and wears himself out. The girl, coldly keeping her decision to herself, continues to be grounded and yelled at. The young man may go to prison. Are these brave decisions worthwhile? It is more real to say that they are valid decisions. They are true to the persons making them, for in the making the persons are being true to themselves. The decisions are based upon a real, not an arbitrary, set of values, for they are the young people's own. The parents' values, the draft board's values, no matter how real they may be to those holding them, cannot be anything but arbitrary to young people who do not—cannot—recognize them as real for themselves. Real decisions must be acknowledged and honored, even though they cannot always be followed. Young people, given acknowledgment and respect, can appreciate that, too. Real decisions have led to self-respect, and they have added an increment of dignity to the deciders. They have solved a problem, which is more than enough to validate them.

There is much that we, as authorities of one kind or another, can do to help young people assume responsibility, to make the brave decisions that will validate their identities (and our influence). We can trust them and give them responsibilities and treat them with respect and humor. We can give them the examples of how we ourselves make decisions. We can teach them to appreciate their own complexity, their own polarities, by responding nonjudgmentally to the whole spectrum of their personalities and their reactions—their generosities as well as their stinginesses, their hits as well as their misses. We commit a serious error when we "type" a young person. It is no more or less than another version of name-calling, and it hurts the person we type as immature, hippie, etc., just as it hurt him years earlier when we called him lazy, selfish, etc.

We can recognize, with Barrett, that a single reaction may express more than one emotion. We can show young people that there are many solutions, not just *our* solution, to any problem. We can be as impatient with dependence as with rebellion. We can articulate for them that they are facing choices and will continue to do so all their lives. We can show them, in our own choice-making, that it is exciting and rewarding to do so. We can react to them as persons of today, not yesterday, when they and things were different. We can let them know of contingency—that there are things, frightening things, that neither they nor we can control. Implicit in all the above, of course, are all the things they *can* control, and we can articulate these, too.

But we must want to avoid the errors of mistrust, of typing, of oversimplifying. We must want to communicate our faith in our youngsters, for we also must want to communicate faith in ourselves to ourselves. It is, essentially, the   who has lost faith in himself who most lacks   hild. We must want, we *do* want, faith   we must not want to go on livin   ing to show this faith   though, because of impossible.

III:
Paradoxes of Parenthood

The authentic child—the one who develops, according to his own nature, in freedom—and the authentic parent—the one who allows his child to develop in freedom—are relatively unencumbered with blocks to free development. It is not that these authentic persons are especially favored by the fates, who have arranged an obstacle-free course through life for them. It is rather that they have been able to recognize a sizable majority of these blocks for what they are: semantic hangups; self-imposed restrictions bearing no relationship at all to real restrictions; inherent contradictions in thinking about and reacting to others. Recognizing these blocks as illogical and unfair generalizations; as brakes on behavior that might very well, unbraked, be appropriate; as residuals from past interpersonal relationships that, once analyzed, have no relationship to present relationships, the authentic person can surmount, virtually transcend, these blocks. He can look at the other—his parent or his child—freely. He can see the other as he is, not as a "type" or a representative of other-ness, of something alien, someone to protect oneself against. It is the perception of one's child in his essence, as he is, as he exists here and now, that, more than anything else parents can do, allows the child to develop in freedom.

The blocks to such clear perception are the para-doxes of parenthood. Paradoxes of childhood exist, too, in abundance. But it is more in the nature of a child to think paradoxically, and hence be less ame-nable to change and control. It is important for us, as parents, to be mature and tolerant enough to allow our children to think paradoxically, even as we try our rigorous best to eliminate paradoxes from our own thinking. We will help our children, if we succeed, to eliminate paradoxes from *their* thinking that much sooner.

A paradox is a contradiction, and for the present purpose it can be considered as a logical and emo-tional contradiction between the way we, as parents, perceive ourselves and the way we perceive our chil-dren. Our thinking is prey to unlimited paradoxes and contradictions, many of which are particularly de-structive in our efforts to establish free relationships with our children.

It has long seemed to me that a wide, often danger-ous and sometimes unbridgeable gap separates our perceptions of ourselves from our perceptions of others. To me, I am a fascinating creature of unlimited complexity. My fantasies are immeasurably rich, my reactions fascinatingly unpredictable, my behavior unguessably subtle, my feelings deep and intense, my thoughts so profound as to be as often as not beyond articulation. Yet I can dismiss everyone else with a word—"lazy," "intellectual," "conceited," "hysterical." And occasionally, with an unpleasant start, I find myself, in all my diversity, similarly but oh, so unfairly, pinpointed by others. "Narcissistic," for some reason, comes to mind.

A seventh-grade girl, walking down the corridor of her junior high school, sees the cutest boy in the eighth grade approaching. She panics, clamps her lips over her braces and practically breaks into a trot as they pass, tossing her head so that he won't see her flushed face, her trembling lips. The wordless encounter safely weathered, she pauses at the door of her classroom and looks back at the boy. Another girl approaches and passes the boy without speaking. Our seventh grader smiles grimly as she walks into class. She thinks, Golly, Becky's sure stuck up.

A wife, wounded and resentful, shoves her tardy husband's steak back in the oven. She broods on his lack of consideration, on the freedom of his life, such that he can stop for a drink with his friends on the way home, while she is chained to house and kitchen. He enters, breathing gin, slaps her affectionately.

She moves away, announces that his steak is over-done, which serves him right, and privately decides there'll be no sex tonight. Her attention is distracted by her four-year-old complaining that his big brother is playing with his favorite toy. "Oh, let him play with it," she snaps. "Honestly, Petey, you're so selfish."

A second paradox disturbs me. It, too, separates us from others, and also seems dangerous and often unbridgeable. It seems to imply: I am active; they are passive. I have control over my behavior. I am re-markably good at understanding the forces that play upon me and upon others, but while I am accordingly able to take them into account, to balance them, and to behave appropriately, others are not. They are dupes or puppets and really have to be protected from the ghastly errors into which they inevitably will fall.

"No, I don't think you should, son. It's too dangerous."

"But, Dad! You did the same thing when you were my age. You told me!"

"That was different."

Like the first paradox—self as complex, others as simple—this one, too, bespeaks lack of empathy. It also pictures the significant block to good relationships with others described in detail by J. F. T. Bugental in his book *The Search for Authenticity.* He refers to it as the "subject-object split," and although he describes this split as occurring internally (Myself as subject—the doer, the agent; I, in contrast to Myself, as object—the passive recipient, the puppet, Me), I do not think it violates Bugental's idea to adapt it to a self-other relationship. It seems most sensible to ask when something has gone wrong between oneself and another person—one's child in particular, but it applies to any relationship—"Am I treating him as if he were an object, something (not someone) to be manipulated, or something who has been manipulated?" The parent who violently blames the unhealthy influence of his teen-ager's friends as being totally responsible for the boy's or the girl's troubles is treating his child as though he or she was an object. The youngster may agree (the authentic one won't), but he will resent being so treated, and he will move even farther away from his parent.

We resent being considered dupes; in our culture, it is perhaps one of the worst insults of all to be called a sucker, and most of us will go to fantastic heights of rationalization to deny being thought a fool. Our rationalizations, however, are almost immediately seen through by anyone halfway paying attention to us. Most people don't bother to figure things out, we think, so the transparency of our rationalizations is conveniently opaqued by this very paradox—the one

that says "I'm not fooling myself with this rationalization, but I'm sure putting it over on everyone else."
We teach our children our own fears: to be considered naïve, to be considered gullible, to be a figure
of scorn and contempt, to have others laugh at us—
there is nothing worse, and we accordingly teach
our children, by our example, to bluff, to rationalize,
to lie, to play it cool, and never, never to expose
legitimate curiosity, honest questioning, or spontaneous feeling. Madison Avenue has long played on our
fears of being "out of it"; we have long revered
comedians who play the simple fool, thereby allowing us to feel sophisticated.

Hating and fearing this exposure of ourselves so
much, then, why do we call our children dupes,
pawns of others, and thus ensure their resentment of
us, even as we resented our own parents when they
did the same thing to us? It is a part of the "I am
active, they are passive; I am subject, they are objects" paradox, and we are going to continue having
trouble with our children until we resolve it. The
resolution is simple: They are active, too; they are
subjects, also; and they, like us, have the identical
and very basic resentments against being considered
anything else.

A third contradictory parental practice we indulge
in without thought, similar to the others in its denial
of the fact that our children have the same feelings
we do, centers on the infliction of pain. It is cruelty

at its most highly developed degree, and it takes place constantly. Listen: A little boy, lips trembling in pain and anger, faces his mother defiantly and announces that he's going to run away. "O.K.," the mother invariably replies—one thinks of Pavlov's dogs, drooling mindlessly and inappropriately every time a bell rings —"Go ahead. I'll help you pack." The little boy is defeated. Having tried in vain to get some compassion from the woman who just beat him up, he finds she is truly implacable. Something hardens in him. Perhaps it is the same boy, a dozen years later, who, interrogating a captured North Vietnamese woman suspected of being an informant to the Viet Cong, becomes irritated with her uncooperativeness and pushes her out of the helicopter in which they are flying. This handsome young man, his hair cut short, the picture of wholesome young American manhood, tells his adventure with his white teeth flashing in merriment. Yes, he may well be the same boy whose mother, in the instance recounted and in countless others, so hardened him with her deliberate cruelty that he could enjoy telling of the rag-fluttering, flailing, screaming fall of the old woman down into the jungle.

Is this callous mother who so self-righteously denies her little boy's intense, if ill-advised, plea for some compassion the same one who complains to her husband throughout dinner and for the rest of the evening about the cold shoulder and the curt monosyllable she received that morning at the supermarket from the doctor's wife? Yes, it is. She is not insensitive to cruelty herself; yet she inflicts it systematically upon her children (and, this evening, upon her husband).

The reason for the cold shoulder may possibly be the call this mother put in to the doctor very late the night before. Her son had climbed high in a tree and refused to come down. Throughout dinner, which his parents ate with exaggerated relish in the boy's sight, remarking frequently and fatuously upon the particular delights of the meal, he clung stubbornly to his limb, far too high for his father to climb after him. They tried, the mother whined frantically to the doctor hours later, "everything." "Everything" meant threats, bribery, cajolery, lies, warnings, and screams. "We told him he'd fall and hurt himself. We told him we'd call the fire department, and the firemen would say what a baby he was. We told him he'd catch cold and get sick. We told him there were owls in the tree that would peck his eyes out. We told him he'd get thrashed within an inch of his life if he didn't come down, and we told him he could stay up and watch the Late Show if he did come down. We've tried *everything!*"

"Did you tell him simply that you wanted him to come down because you loved him and wanted him to be with you?" the doctor asked.

"Well, no," she said and called back a moment

later to say that the boy, who had been waiting for five hours to hear just this, had come right down.

The next time she saw her doctor she complained that her husband never told her he loved her any more. It is to be assumed that she learned nothing from her son's tree-sitting episode.

It is also to be assumed that very few of us are ignorant of the Golden Rule. This is the resolution, simple, basic, time-tested, to the paradox of inflicting cruelty upon our children while seeing it bring out the worst in ourselves when we experience it. "Thou shalt not take vengeance, nor bear any grudge against the children of thy people, but thou shalt love thy neighbor as thyself. . . ."

In doing unto our children that which we would have done to ourselves, we are laying a base for the compassion and human feeling in these children that will bring them social and personal rewards for the rest of their lives. We are spreading antidotes to the callousness and coldness with which we treat not just prisoners of war, but our old people and our poor people and our tempest-tossed. It is not only the Spanish Inquisition or the Children's Crusades or the witch hunts or the crematoria for Europe's Jews that demonstrate man's fiendish cruelty to his fellow man. It is in the homes of respectable families where such massive programs of torture are born. The prizing of human feeling, as embodied in the Golden Rule, can abort these monstrous births.

IV:

The Authentic Child

We do not know the object by conquering and subduing it but rather by letting it be what it is and, in letting it be, allowing it to reveal itself as what it is.

—Heidegger

By substituting "the child" for "the object" in the above quotation, and by following through with personal instead of impersonal pronouns, the first step toward understanding the child has been taken.

Let us look next at another authority, John Anderson, who, in 1948, started a quiet revolution in child psychology with his description of the child as:

> ... an active energy system coping with and creating his world—not at all a passive organism victimized by stimuli from his environment. ... [He] responds selectively, ignoring as well as attending to stimuli. His past is largely forgotten, and he lives in a present where he retains from his previous experiences those events which have been repeatedly encountered in the form of cultural val-

ues, persistent family attitudes and problems, and in general the more or less successful patterns of adjustment. . . . [He] evidences resiliency and a substantial capacity for tolerating and recovering from stresses and frustrations.

Anderson takes a strongly existential stand here, concentrating upon the child's present (here and now) adjustment, only *relatively* influenced by his past. He emphasizes the coping, active, adjusting nature of the child, who is far more than a passive pawn of circumstance. And he describes the sentient, intelligent, "resilient" character of the child—who is, in these traits, not so different from what we like to think of ourselves. Above all, Anderson, on a firm empirical basis, is applauding the child's extraordinary capacity to recover, undiscouraged, from adverse familial and cultural pressure. For parents, it is a heartening statement.

A second step has been taken. Understanding the child comes from letting him show us what he is like. Conversely, the more we try to "conquer and subdue," or mold, or influence, the less well are we going to understand him.

Is it important to understand the child, especially if the corollary may seem to be to let him run wild without subduing or influencing him? Yes. Listen, in their own words, to three- and twelve- and sixteen- and twenty-one-(and thirty-six and eighty-eight) year-olds, all saying, "Understand me!" Yes, it is very important.

The corollary to letting a child reveal himself without coercion is not to let him "run wild." The understood child has no need to run wild, for running wild is simply one of his ways of saying, "Understand me!"

The corollary is that the child gets an enormous boost, a "head start," toward authenticity. The other requisite is loving him. Erikson says, ". . . man can activate man and be activated by him in [such] a way that the binding forces of Eros become operative."

The mutual activation between people, such that each loves the other more, is a common experience, but it can never become too common. It ranges from the upward revision of our opinion of another person's taste upon receiving a compliment from him to the fierce and growing passion of lovers locked in naked, defenseless intimacy. Between parent and child, mutual activation is an experience of love and communion that might be called, after Bugental, the "growthful encounter." It is an encounter that leads to growth in the relationship and, here and now, to a delightful warmth of intimacy at the very moment of its being. It is instigated by the parent's spontaneously voiced pleasure in the child—something he's drawn, or done, the way he looks, or just his being there; or, perhaps more often, it is instigated by the child's spontaneous, "I love you, Mommy," or "You're pretty cool, Dad." A full response by the other, equally spontaneous, equally loving, is the condition for full activation.

Eros is the driving force of love. It is inseparable from letting a child reveal himself. Parents tell themselves and anyone who will listen (other coercive parents are the ones most willing to listen and have their pressure tactics legitimized and reinforced) that they "conquer and subdue" out of love, but they do not. They pressure and push and "guide" and "discipline" out of fear. They fear that their own hated impulses will break out in their children. They fear what the neighbors will say. They fear that allowing the child to reveal himself will lead automatically and inevitably to delinquency, crime, immorality and poor manners, in spite of centuries of evidence that just the reverse is the case.

The parent who really loves his child will *of course* —as a matter of course—allow the child's self-revelation, at the child's own pace and when the child feels so moved. He will regard the prevailing opinion that duress is necessary without feeling in the least bit threatened—indeed, with amusement—because it is so evident to him that his child—understood and allowing himself to be more and more deeply understood all the time, loved and loving, and increasingly so both ways—already has the inner discipline that is a hallmark of the authentic child. This child simply does not need to be conquered. There are so many more interesting and worthwhile things to be doing with and for the child, that pressuring him, with its consequent balkings and resentments, is, among other things, a frightful waste of time.

The parents who love and listen to their children believe very strongly in discipline. It is the same kind of discipline with which they order and govern their own lives, a substantial part of which is devoted to their chief responsibility: the children. The mother who, out of financial need or adherence to a narcissistic "feminine mystique," and the father who, out of work pressures or long-lived resentment at having his bachelorhood or his honeymoon interrupted by the children, devote only minimal time to their children are abjuring and denying their chief responsibility. Inauthentic themselves, they are creating inauthentic children who will, in the course of time, probably continue the process with *their* children. This is not, of course, to say that all working mothers or all harassed fathers are automatically inauthentic. Indeed, many if not most of them are superior parents because, recognizing their chief responsibilities, they so richly compensate to their children for the time necessarily spent away from them that the children are even better off. It is those parents whose outside activities are chiefly aimed toward letting them "get away from the kids for a while" who do serious injustice to their children.

The discipline that authentic parents support is not the superficial kind that exclusively emphasizes punitive measures. The behavior of the original disciples, before and after their Lord's death, is hardly the kind of behavior likely to have been inspired by threats, spankings, humiliation, deprivation, isolation, bribery, etc.—all imposed from without and all representative of how the inauthentic parent would define "discipline."

Does a young person elect to go to graduate school and proceed to make an original contribution to the world's knowledge in his chosen field because he was pushed and prodded and pressured to do his homework throughout his first twelve grades, or because he came, through identifying with his parents' delighted interest in their own learning as well as his— plus, if he was very lucky, having perhaps one good teacher in all those years—to love the excitement of learning so much that he didn't need to be pushed, prodded and pressured?

Real discipline, as Jesus so masterfully demonstrated, validated by his "children's" later achievements, is respecting, listening, trusting, and loving. It is guiding and inspiring. It is being generous. It is providing daily intimate opportunities for identification and emulation of one's own behavior by the young. It is a richness of giving. It is a far cry from the negative and poverty-stricken armamentarium of the inauthentic and stingy parent: punishment, humiliation, deprivation, and isolation.

Now, for the second step: Anderson's description of *any* child has shown us how it is possible that loving and listening to a child are the first steps toward his authenticity. The child, he tells us—though any five-minute period of unbiased observation of any living child will tell us the same thing—as a coping, creating energy system, is equipped through his many strengths and assets to display, creatively, his resiliency and his "substantial capacity for tolerating and recovering from stresses and frustrations."

The child we are beginning to understand is an admirable creature. He deserves being listened to; he is worthy of being loved. He has within himself the seed of future compassion and creativity. He is, here and now, fascinating, forgiving, loving, and funny. He is masterful, but he is understanding; he is responsive, and he is resilient. He doesn't waste time brooding about the past or unduly fantasizing about the future, but can approach the present moment with a zest and a total commitment that makes the present moment worth all the world's treasures. He is happy, though he is, of course, sad and unhappy at times. He is, above all, himself. To be oneself, and not to fear being oneself, is a joyous and freeing experience. It consists of a confident spontaneity, a courageous willingness to try out one's powers—verbal, physical, social, intellectual—and to try on one's feelings. The child who is himself sizes himself in situations and with persons he encounters, and if he fails—if things don't work out—he is not prevented from trying again the next time. In every self-sizing, or self-testing, the child learns a little more about himself; he takes another step toward identity. He, unlike adults who restrict their behavior to stereo-typed role-playing, is not afraid to be himself in all his complexity, expressing all his many and often contradictory facets.

He is the authentic child. He has no mystic quality of character or temperament, no special fortune in his selection of parents and grandparents. There is not even an unidentifiable "something" in his makeup, such as a special aptitude for mathematics or art, that in any way sets him apart from any other child. He is every child—real, spontaneous, natural, himself, honest, happy, open in his reactions—both positive and negative—and free to be all these. The authentic child is himself, he is free to be himself, and he is blessed with parents who willingly and gladly offer him countless opportunities wherein he can be himself.

Every child is born authentic. It is a desperate thing to see so many of them spoiled and spoiling into inauthenticity.

V:
A Richness of Giving

Contrary to the rationalist tradition, we now know that it is not his reason that makes man man, but rather that reason is a consequence of that which really makes him man. For it is man's existence as a self-transcending self that has forged and formed reason as one of its projects.

—Barrett

"You just can't *reason* with that child!"

No, you can't reason with that or any other child. You can't reason with many adults, for that matter. "Come, let us reason together," like so many bromides, sounds fine and may even be effective in making us think, for a while, that we are reasoning. But what actually happens is the imposition of the stronger set of values and prejudices upon the unhappy weaker set. Indeed, it is a point of honor with most adults *not* to be amenable to reasoning, for this somehow implies weakness, faltering allegiance to their own values and prejudices, and therefore inconceivable. Many of us would consider ourselves traitors to our upbringing, to consider seriously that there is anything of value in the Beatles' music or hair styles, no matter how passionately *and* reasonably presented by our teen-agers. Yet we are honestly injured—and thereafter, dishonestly vindictive—when these teen-agers "refuse" to reason (*i.e.*, adopt our prejudices) concerning good music and attractive hair styles. Some gained the impression that President Johnson saw the increasingly substantial segment of the population that disagreed with him regarding the Vietnam war as a mob of unreasonable and dangerous teen-agers. Perhaps the frustration felt by these deeply responsible adults, whose attempts to get the administration to alter or at least to review its stand on the war were so consistently thwarted or appeared so fruitless, is akin to the frustration felt by our teen-agers as they attempt to deal with us.

No, you can't reason with that child if your reasoning consists of the attempt to impose your own values on him. You can reason with him, however, if reasoning is defined as a mutual problem-solving situation. Children have brains and intelligence just as adults have. They also have passions and emotions, and these speak much louder in the conduct of their affairs than does the cooler voice of reason. Indeed, our most inauthentic moments may be those of our strongest insistence upon the primacy of reason over passion. Perhaps we have a deep fear of primitivity, of abandon, of our animal urges, and, Aristotelians still, we proclaim our rationality the louder, to try to silence the intrusive and, it seems, disruptive and discordant voice of emotion. The authentic parent grants the dominance of passion in his children, because he does not fear—indeed, he enjoys—the illogical but gratifying expressions of his own passions. You can't reason with a child, or anyone else, if you ignore these lusty, penetrating cries from his heart and from your own. "The heart has its reasons," we need to remind ourselves, "of which reason knows not."

There often seems a gap, vast and unbridgeable, between these two sets of reasons, the heart's and the mind's, and it often seems to many parents that the way to bridge the gap is to destroy altogether the incautious, threatening impulses of the heart. Productive reasoning, when it takes place (yes, you *can* reason with that child), considers and integrates the two sets of reasons, and it is a deeply intimate and satisfying process. It is the kind of thinking Heidegger has in mind when he says, "Thinking only begins at the point where we have come to know that Reason, glorified for centuries, is the most obstinate adversary of thinking."

Consider the four-year-old who won't go to bed, the nine-year-old who won't wear her glasses, the thirteen-year-old who won't cut his hair, the fifteen-year-old who won't obey the curfew laws and whose

jeans are far too tight,* the any-year-old who won't
do his homework. (While you're at it, consider the
thirty- and forty-year-olds who won't stop drinking or
smoking or being unfaithful.) Some of these re-
fusals are more unreasonable than others, but all of
them seem totally unresponsive to at least the nar-
rower definition of reasoning, namely, the attempted
imposition of the concerned person's values upon the
recalcitrant one.

The broader definition may offer some hope, for it
includes consideration of the dark forces that are so
strong and sticky a part of the obdurate behavior.
These forces are referred to as the Furies, after their
personifications in the *Oresteia,* by Barrett, who says:

> The Furies are really to be revered and not simply
> bought off; in fact, they cannot be bought off (not
> even by our modern tranquilizers and sleeping
> pills) but are to be placated only through being
> given their just and due respect. They are the
> darker side of life, but in their own way as holy as
> the rest. Indeed, without them there would be no
> experience of the holy at all. Without the shudder
> of fear or the trembling of dread man would never
> be brought to stand face to face with himself or his
> life. . . .

---

* . . . for youth no less becomes
  The light and careless livery that it wears
  Than settled age his sables and his weeds, . . .
  —*Hamlet,* IV, 7

You can reason with that child, but not distort that reasoning; the discussion should be an interchange of ideas and opinions leading to new, unpredicted ideas and opinions. It is false, both on the part of the parent and on the part of the child, to label as reasoning something which is not reasoning. If you give orders, if you impose values and prejudices, if you direct and control your child's behavior, then acknowledge it as such, and he will respect you much more. And you will feel genuine frustration if it doesn't work, and genuine self-respect if it does. It is one thing to be frustrated in honest purpose: "I'm not reasoning with you, young lady; I'm *telling* you!" Whereupon she does as she pleases. But she knows where you stand, and after she has tested her stand, and yours, she can make her own choice thereafter. One hopes it won't be too late, and it is likely that it will not be.

It is another thing to be frustrated in devious purpose. Frustration that results from the honest opposition of two strong minds can be productive. The frustration that is caused by a dishonest attempt to clothe a command in the cloak of "reason" leads only to more and more frustration, each stage becoming murkier and more destructive along the way. There is nothing dishonest in telling a child what to do. It is dishonest only if it is not presented as a command but instead, in cowardly fashion, as something else.

"Reasoning" therefore fails if it is not reasoning.

"Reasoning" also fails if it is over-determined; if the admittedly difficult, complex task of sharing ideas and opinions across the generation barrier is brought to bear unnecessarily upon an issue too trivial to warrant such an overkill. A four-year-old's refusal to go to bed can much more easily be handled by firmness. A fourteen-year-old's hair style is much more harmoniously handled by humor (and if father's humor is more sarcastic than gentle, well, it's still better than raging and blowing). In neither of these cases is the child's behavior destructive, actually or potentially, to himself or to others. Furthermore, in neither case is the behavior amenable to reasoning, being governed on the one hand by pre-logical drives toward independence, and on the other hand by alogical drives toward peer-acceptance. If your child is trapped, by virtue of being four or fourteen, into such behavior, consider the traps of adulthood and the equally illogical behavior expected of you, and complied with. Consider also that there are many children, even as there are many adults, who can see the traps and thereupon comply with them or not, as a matter of choice. The child, and the adult, who chooses to conform or not to conform must be acknowledged. In the acknowledgment, and the consequent reinforcement of intelligent decision-making behavior, lies the groundwork for real reasoning.

Real reasoning is a process, difficult and complex, entered into by two or more persons in good faith, of common positive regard for one another, in which both parties have complete freedom of verbal behavior and as complete freedom of physical behavior as is practically, legally, financially, and morally realistic. The reality of a curfew is different from, and much more compelling than, the reality of a parent's anxiety. Youngsters, who are arch-realists, respond to the impersonality of the former, and test, resist, resent, and grow miserably guilty about the tyranny of the latter.

Reasoning, then, can take place only when two conditions are met: open channels of communication between the reasoners, in which honesty and self-disclosure ("These are my motives in talking to you like this . . .") are characteristic of both; and the assurance of freedom of behavior on the part of both reasoners. If the child or the father feels beaten before he starts—if no matter what he says, his father or his son still won't relent—then the reasoning has degenerated into something other than reasoning even before it starts. The parent who cavils at these prerequisites—who says, "Communication is O.K., but freedom of behavior isn't. Communication means she's perfectly free to go out and get pregnant? No, sir!"—this parent does not understand that the result of such reasoning, with such prerequisites, is choice-making on the part of both.

After such a conference, with the necessary requirements, it is possible to choose on the basis of improved understanding between one's own and the opposing point of view. An encounter has been made —with oneself, with one's child or parent—and the result of a significant encounter is always a reevaluation or a new appraisal of oneself and one's behavior. Then, if she still goes out and gets pregnant, which she is free to do, and which she would have done anyhow without the encounter with you, it might well, from some points of view at least, be the best decision for her. Under most ordinary circumstances, however, the possibility that she will not get pregnant (or even have sexual intercourse) is high.

The use of terms like "possibility" and "probability" may seem ominous. Even though we recognize its impossibility, we want surety in our moments of worry, of inauthenticity; we want a guarantee that by following certain modes of behavior, our daughters will not become pregnant. We may conclude, as a result of recognizing contingency, of recognizing that surety is a myth, that existentialism leads to immoral, destructive choice-making, just as we earlier may have concluded that permissiveness automatically created a "spoiled" child.

A juvenile court judge has recently asked for funds to finance a program designed to educate parents not to be "permissive" with their children on the grounds that such "permissiveness" is the reason for the backbreaking and heartbreaking load of cases on his bench. This seems to us biased and almost irrational, considering that even a cursory reading of the juveniles' folders would show at once that their background consists far more of brutality and restrictiveness than of "permissiveness." The judge has perhaps confused abandonment and ignoring of the child with permissiveness, and if so, we can simply but sharply admonish him to define his terms more clearly. But it is more likely that the judge, who is a careful thinker as well as a humane man, is reacting to the formidable, coronary-attack-provoking task before him: that of imposing discipline upon undisciplined youngsters. One can easily see, and can sympathize with the judge, how he might long for precedent discipline, and how he might easily assume that its absence is what makes his task so hard.

The worried parent fears that an existential approach to his defiant daughter which clearly states that the choice of whether or not to become pregnant is up to her, after she has had the opportunity to discuss the alternatives with her parent in an atmosphere of reasonableness and non-pressure, is a sick thing and will allow the girl to go ahead and do what she wants to. He underestimates the strength of allowing decisions after relatively full knowledge of oneself is obtained. He insults his daughter in denying her the ability to see what is best for her. He insults himself in denying his influence, throughout her growing years, upon her decision-making.

Worse can be said about the parent who denies his daughter choice in the matter of her relationship with boys. It is a sick footnote, but it must be added. This parent—the father every bit as much as the mother—identifies himself with his daughter's sexuality. He is the father who, years ago in his lusty adolescence, said, "I wish I was a girl: I'd lay every guy who came around." He was clearly projecting his own urgent sexuality when he said that. Indeed he was looking for a laugh, but he was really unconsciously expressing his quite normal adolescent bisexuality. And he was a frustrated kid, finding in the fantasy of a willing girl an outlet for the needs so cruelly and, it then seemed permanently, denied him.

The mother's motives are less murky: she forbids her daughter to do the very thing she herself most wishes to do. By denying her daughter's needs, she denies her own, and she thereby maintains her self-image as a proper matron. The young men who cluster around her daughter are an attractive and sexy lot. Her husband may be less, far less, than ardent, and though she lives her days in warmth and good works, she gets far less than she gives. She is understandably, but covertly, resentful.

It is a simple thing to say to this father and to this mother, "You are simply indulging yourselves, your

49

own clandestine needs, in denying freedom of choice to your daughter. You do not fear what will happen to her; you fear the exciting release of your own long-suppressed desires." It is not so simple for the father and the mother to understand this, for even in these post-Freudian days of sophistication the defenses against our own sexual needs are strong. We must first understand ourselves, communicate honestly with ourselves, before we can presume to communicate with our children.

Communication, freedom, and encounter: these are the key words and processes involved in reasoning. The results are benign and constructive; the relationship between the participants is elevated to new heights of intimacy and understanding. It can take place when one of the participants is at least seven years old (if the other one is older), and it is something for which we all hunger. It helps us stand face to face with ourselves and our lives; without this open confrontation we and our lives would be empty indeed.

VI:
The Element of Dread

For the choice in . . . human situations is almost never between a good and an evil, where both are plainly marked as such and the choice therefore made in all the certitude of reason; rather, it is between rival goods, where one is bound to do some evil either way, and where the ultimate outcome and even—or most of all—our own motives are unclear to us. The terror of confronting oneself in such a situation is so great that most people panic and try to take cover under any universal rule that will apply, if only it will save them from the task of choosing themselves.

—Barrett

"All right, young man, you eat your dinner, or there'll be no dessert. Make up your mind."

"It's up to you, dear, you know. If you don't do your homework, you'll never get to a good college."

"What are you going to major in?"

There is an element of dread in each of these choices. Kierkegaard writes that dread is the sight of the self, a "yawning abyss," without attachment, that

prevents one from becoming truly free in his choice-
and decision-making. Whether one is deciding to go
steady or not, or whether to study or to spend the evening on the telephone, or what to choose as a career,
it is the element of dread—the vision of oneself, un-
protected, vulnerable, liable to shameful exposure—
that keeps the choice from being a free one.

It is one thing to point out the element of dread. It
is quite another thing to recognize it as such, as har-
rowing, frightening, self-involving. We—and, because of the examples we set, our children—do not
want to experience dread. We accordingly drive our
choice-making into an irrealistic realm of pure rationality. We make lists of pros and cons; we ask advice
of authorities; we follow the examples of others, ignoring our individuality. The only reason the choices
we make according to these procedures sometimes
work out for the best is that we are constructed psychologically in a way which ensures that whatever we
decide upon is, ultimately, the best.

It probably isn't, though. The choices we make on
the basis of sheer reason, without recognizing the element of dread, are bound to be limited and limiting
ones. Unwilling to recognize, much less accept, his
feelings of inadequacy, a young man of exceptional
capacity takes a position as a probation officer after
his graduation from college instead of applying for
law school. To be a probation officer is a good enough
thing: it is important, and it may be occupationally

fulfilling to the young man. It is, however, a job whose satisfaction can be largely determined by the attitudes and practices of the judge for whom he works. In other words, in his choice of probation as a career, the young man is taking a chance that he will have a decent, equitable judge on the bench who will recognize and respect the young man's professionalism. There is enough evidence pointing toward the increasing closed-mindedness of men in administrative and authoritative positions to make the chance the young man is taking more of a possibility than a probability. If he has enough insight to know that he would be essentially happier—that is, more secure, less vulnerable to doubts as to his adequacy on the job—with the probability of a closed-minded boss, who may be more apt to judge a juvenile offender on the basis of his own biases than on the basis of the probation officer's report, then his choice of probation as a career is a well-founded one. He can, after all, spend his evenings bitching to his wife about the unreasonableness of the judge. If her image of wifeliness is to listen sympathetically to her husband's complaints, then everything is bound to work out swimmingly.

There are too many if's in this scheme. It is more likely that an intelligent and reasonably ambitious young man will not be happy in such a situation, that his wife will become increasingly restive listening to his complaints, and that he will increasingly take out his disappointment and self-attacks in not having gone to law school in the first place on his wife, his children, and his job.

It may well be, in other words, that a far wiser choice for the young man would have been law school, with its promise of a long working career relatively free from direction from above. Assuming the young man is intellectually and motivationally capable of handling the demands of law school, he would do well to look into the yawning abyss of himself, with the mirrored insecurities and inadequacies he sees there and the intellectual and motivational strengths as well. If the young man is able to say, "I fear, but I want," then the "reasonable" objections of having a wife and children, having already spent four years in school, the settling down of his friends, and all the other practical reasons for getting a job as soon as possible will fall into place. They will be consequential reasons influencing his decision, but they will not be the determining ones. The determining factor will be whether the "I fear" or the "I want" predominates in his clear look at himself. The choice here is a simple one. It is significant and interesting, at this point, that knowledge of the causes of the "I fear" syndrome—past failures, parental reinforcement of failures as a child, and the like—has very little, if anything, to do with the young man's decision.

A mother walked into the playroom of my office

one day, where her son had been throwing darts. She looked at the five darts sticking in the target, at the one on the floor, and said, "You missed one, didn't you?" I suspect that this boy would not find it easy to apply for law school in the future even if he wished to.

The young man may have total insight into the causes of his fear and yet remain impotent and indecisive when it comes to making the choice. Counseling, advice, psychotherapy, or whatever may be designed to illuminate the causal factors will be ineffective unless it also helps the young man look squarely at his present dread. Insight therapy alone leads only to intellectual understanding. The immediate—existential—experience of encountering one's fears leads to choice and then to action. The action, furthermore, is appropriate action, because it is undertaken in freedom.

We can help our youngsters, of whatever age, encounter their selves-in-fear. It is not done by emphasizing the consequences of untaken action, as was the case in the quotations at the beginning of this chapter. It is done, and with astonishing success, by allowing the youngster to recognize and accept his doubts, without denial or shame, through our own empathic, nonjudgmental acceptance.

The secret of a successful relationship—parent-child, marital, or any other—is to expose and to articulate, to express one's own feelings in any delicate or potentially explosive situation without going on to judge, to criticize, or to direct the other person. There is a vast difference between saying, "It makes me sick to see you drunk every night. It's disgusting; cut it out!" and saying, "It makes me sick to see you drunk every night." In the first case, the offender is almost obliged to defend himself. This leads to counterattack, and a battle is well on its way—to end unproductively in sullenness or a black eye and still unresolved mutual resentments. The simple expression of one's feelings, on the other hand, gives no opportunity for defensiveness, because there is no attack against which to defend. It may stir up guilt in the listener, but this is often necessary to mobilize his sense of responsibility. In any event, it is an honest communication, and it does not lend itself to vicious, sterile attempts at self-justification and counterattacks. Husbands and wives do well to subscribe to this approach to communication and problem-solving. Parents can, with equal prospects of success, use the approach to help their children assess themselves, their impact upon others, and their enormous potentialities. From such assessment comes responsible decision-making and appropriate action. (Some parents, after a few years of being ignored by their offspring, figure that the kids mean it when they say they don't care *what* the parents think about their behavior. The kids don't mean it. They do care, and it's worthwhile, if initially discouraging, at least to operate on the assumption that they do.)

Gene, Bob, and Phil are three personable, bright recent college graduates in their early twenties. Their trouble is that they don't know what to do next. Their undergraduate major, psychology, has prepared them only for graduate work, for which they all have the grades and the intelligence. They are not at all sure that they want to spend another four or five years in school to earn the doctorate without which work as a psychologist is limited in responsibility, freedom, and salary. Gene tried graduate work for a semester but dropped out, still unconvinced that this was the field he wanted to be in the rest of his life. Bob is in training to sell insurance, and Phil is chaperoning a busload of high school kids around the country for the summer. Both have yet to decide whether or not to come back to school in the fall. None is facing induction—Gene, the oldest, has served already. Bob is exempt as a sole surviving son and Phil is unqualified on the basis of a mild heart murmur.

Each of them asks, "Can you help me in my decision? Can vocational or interest or personality tests help? Why can't I decide what I want to do?" Somehow they feel ashamed, at their age and with their college degrees, not to have made a decision about the course of their future lives. They are not frivolous or thoughtless; they have already demonstrated dili-

gence and application. They are not emotionally un-
stable, and they are not without insight or well-
developed identities. They are feeling pressure within
themselves to make a decision, but none feels really
panicked about it. They all want to get married,
though none has a special girl in mind, but they are
sensible enough to want to establish themselves occupationally first. Besides, they are all attractive and
lusty young men, and they suffer very little from
sexual frustration.

Their fathers and their professors, no matter how
close they are to them or how much they respect
them, are of very little help, even though they try
their conscientious best to be. These men did not experience the kind of doubting the boys are going
through, and, to be frank, do not have a great deal of
patience with it. They were Depression children, and
their fathers' troubles were influential in their seeking, and deciding upon, whatever opportunity seemed
the most secure. For the most part, they did well, and
their sons and students have not lacked for either
necessities or luxuries. The two generations are very
far apart, and even their mutual respect and good
will are not enough to bridge the apartness. With less
good will, they would label each other: dissolute and
unreliable on the one hand; stuffy and rigid on the
other.

The fathers and professors differ from the young
men also in the number of choices they faced. The

bewildering array of possibilities for the younger generation creates its own confusion, of course, and it, too, is a kind of confusion with which their elders have relatively little experience or understanding— or patience.

These three fine young men, in short, are in existential crises, marked by unclear goals, numerous vague opportunities, and unformed motivational patterns. The results of interest and personality tests tell them only what they already know. Their fathers and professors try to impose their own patterns of choice and success upon the boys. The boys' individualities cannot accept these impositions, even while recognizing that they may be right or wise. They are too bright to "take cover under any universal rule," for they would be the first to recognize, and reject, the hypocrisy and unreality of such a protection.

When Gene came to recognize his crisis and its aspects, he made a decision: to drop out of his only occasionally stimulating graduate course and to take off. He went to Hawaii, got a job as a bartender, and began thinking and experiencing more freely than he had ever been able to before. Bob, upon spelling out his crisis, found it suddenly quite easy to decide to enroll in graduate school, while specializing on the side in selling insurance policies designed for college students. Phil found it just as easy to decide against graduate school (although of the three, he seemed most temperamentally and intellectually suited for it) and to accept the most attractive of the job offers available to him.

Their doubts were by no means resolved by these solutions, and none of them even considers that his solution is anywhere near a permanent one. Each accepts the fact that he may change his mind, maybe reverse himself completely, within a year. But the dread, by facing it as a legitimate and immediate factor in their indecisiveness, has been eliminated. The decisions, for better or worse, were made freely, not in dread, and they are accordingly wise decisions. The boys believe so; their fathers, a bit reluctantly, believe so. To believe in oneself and in one's decisions is important. It is, indeed, vital to an authentic life. It comes from the experience of making free choices: the greater the experience, the stronger the ultimate belief and self-confidence.

We do not have to wait until our sons are graduated from college to help them resolve their crises. They can do it when they're three years old if we have already resolved our own crises. We must have the courage to face dread ourselves, not only to resolve our crises, but to provide a model of crisis-resolution for our sons. If we lack this courage, we have no business being fathers.

VII:
The Stranger
in the Supermarket

If I grow bitterly,
Like a gnarled and stunted tree,
Bearing harshly of my youth
Puckered fruit that sears the mouth;
If I make of my drawn boughs
An inhospitable house,
Out of which I never pry
Towards the water and the sky,
Under which I stand and hide
And hear the day go by outside;
It is that a wind too strong
Bent my back when I was young,
It is that I fear the rain
Lest it blister me again.

—Edna St. Vincent Millay, "Scrub"

It has long been considered—and it still is—that behavior pathology in children and adults has its antecedents in earlier experience, as so movingly articulated by Miss Millay. Behavior pathology does have
its roots in childhood experience, but it is maintained,
and worsened, by current pathogenic conditions.

Hence, the present emphasis upon family therapy when professional help is sought. A child under eighteen or who at any age is still living with his parents, and whose behavior indicates some emotional or behavioral disorder, cannot be treated successfully without as complete participation as possible by his family in the treatment program.

From this step, total family therapy, which has replaced the individual therapy model of therapist and child, the next step seems clear: "therapy" without a therapist. It is the goal of every child therapist so to prepare his patient and his patient's family that they can resume or establish healthy family living without his help or intervention. The question now arises, Are there family living practices that can be learned and pursued that would obviate the need of a therapist in the first place? Yes, there are; and it is the purpose of this chapter to explore the nature, in detail, of such practices. It is not the purpose here to outline therapeutic techniques, except in the broadest sense of the phrase, that can be "practiced" by the parents. For a parent to practice psychotherapy with his children, even assuming that he could do it (which he could not), would be the grossest sort of artificiality. The strength of the parent-child relationship lies in its spontaneity, its lack of artifice. The parent who "uses psychology" on his child is guilty of the worst sort of manipulative chicanery. The child on whom "psychology" is "used" is an unhappy child.

Unfortunately, he often becomes a shrewd and eventually manipulating child—and adult—himself, for he sees through, all too easily and all too quickly, his parents' cheap tactics. A child usually defends himself by adopting his parents' favorite defenses—they are available, after all, and easily emulated—and the conflicts between him and his parents then become deeper, more vicious, and longer-lasting. We do not, as a rule, like people who share our own pathology. To see one's faults in someone else is to despise that person, and to see them in one's own child is to become doubly outraged, for one's child, as an extension of oneself, *is* oneself with doubled faults. There is many a child who has wept and suffered from the punishment inflicted upon him for no other reason than copying his father's or his mother's behavior. The result, tragically, is to reinvoke the punished behavior, thus laying the child open to still more punishment and suffering—and unreasoning hatred of his parents.

A child, particularly one who has such insightless parents, is not able to change this disapproved behavior. He simply tries more of the same, in a vain and sad attempt to become as much like Daddy as possible, so that maybe Daddy won't spank him the next time. Unhappily, this emulation, this identification with the aggressive Daddy, is precisely that behavior designed most effectively to arouse Daddy's wrath all over again, but more the second time. The circle of Daddy's pathology, desperately imitated by the child and leading to more paternal pathology, expressed in beating up the child, becomes more and more vicious. (The use of Daddy here is not to imply that fathers have a monopoly on abusive-defensive punishment. They may with their sons, but mothers are equally culpable, and they impose this insightless cruelty upon their sons and their daughters indiscriminately.)

It is not "psychology" in this cheap, pejorative sense of the word, as a kind of brain-washing technique, that is to be used within a family if a professional therapist is to become unnecessary. The prostitution of "psychology," an honorable discipline, with a respectable academic history and an imposing corpus of knowledge, into a technique for manipulating other people—developed to a high point in the fields of advertising and selling—is, in parent-child relations, more amusing than serious. It apparently consists solely of saying the opposite of what is meant. .

Respect is to be used: the delighted, appreciative loving and honoring of another person close to one. Respect that values his individuality, rejoices in his happiness, and is awed at, almost reverent in the face of, his dignity. Honestly respecting another person—for purposes of discussion here, a child—cannot be called a technique, because it is not an attitude that can be put on, as an actor assumes a role. In a parent of good will, one who welcomes and likes his children, it is an attitude that comes naturally and spontaneously. It is not "practiced." It is an attitude essential to the child's identity-formation, and identity-formation is essential to the child's mental health. It is therefore an important, an essential attitude, this genuine respect for a child, and if a parent does not have it, his child—and he—will pay. They will pay in expensive defense-formation, in continued, insightless punishment and manipulation of those whom they recognize to be like them, of those who share their weakness and who suffer similarly from the worst disease of all: disrespect, of self and others. It cannot be said too often: to respect others, one must first respect oneself. But to respect oneself, one must first have been respected by one's parents, in the ambiguous years of inchoate identity. We are repelled by the sight of a man who so lacks respect for his fellow man that he berates, or spanks, or shoots, or lynches him. He becomes ugly, distorted, inhuman in his actions; and we know at once that he is more to be pitied than his victim. We know that he cannot respect himself, and we are sick for them both. We see the woman in the supermarket, screaming at her child, threatening him with shrill imprecations, and we turn away from so inhuman a spectacle with disgust. Yet we do it ourselves, and in the back of our mind is the thought, All those others out there are watching. They admire me. They know what I'm going through with this brat. They see how wisely I'm teaching him how to adjust.

We deceive ourselves, and we hurt our children. The pity of it is, we don't need to. We can, after all, let our natural feelings of pride and delight in our children, and in ourselves as parents, come to the surface and be seen. We are, of course, too worried about "spoiling" the children—or about having some stranger in the supermarket think we are spoiling them—to allow a natural delight in the children to show. It is, however, a safe guess that this stranger, as long as his opinion is so important, would rather hear endearments than shrieks.

The key then to respecting a child, beyond respecting oneself, is becoming aware of his dignity. It does harm to a child's dignity, or to one's own, to yell at him in public. Dignity is an essential component of identity, and identity, as we know at once by looking within ourselves, is essential to happiness. If I know not who I am, if I am unsure of my very opinions and reactions, much less of my behavior; if I am beset by doubts; if I feel miles off my course and the very moments of my day seem uncharted and aimless; if I am constantly tormented by anxieties about what others think of me, why they haven't called lately, what they're saying about me; if I feel unimportant to others, unable to influence even my children, so that it wouldn't make any difference were I to drop out of sight forever—then I am clearly not happy.

Equally clearly, I have only a fragment of identity, and even that bit is more narcissistic than not. Narcissistic identity is a painful and defensive self-consciousness, a compensatory self-aggrandizement, often in the form of vanity. Healthy identity is refreshingly unselfconscious, although it involves high self-awareness.

High self-awareness, an essential quality of identity, is to be contrasted with the painful self-awareness of a Charlie Brown, turned to stone, miserably aware of his inadequacies, by a glance from the little red-haired girl. An apt contrast to Charlie Brown is our late President John F. Kennedy, whose easy grace in any situation seemed to bespeak the confidence not only of aristocracy but especially of firm inner pride. To watch him in a television film—greeting guests, relaxing with his family, presiding at a press conference—was to be impressed with his reliance upon himself, with his apparent confidence that he could cope with whatever came up rather than relying upon custom or tradition. For most of us, it is important to find out what others think, what they would do, what to wear, what to say in situations likely to be unpredictable. And most of us wish it did not have to be so, that we could, unprepared and unweighted by the rules of the game, react spontaneously to that which befalls us.

We see a child, especially our own child, shy, frightened, stuttering in miserable self-consciousness in a new situation, and we see ourselves. We ache for the child, but we usually worsen his agony by calling attention to it, cruelly: "Don't be so shy." "There's nothing to be afraid of." "My, you are shy, aren't you?"

We wish our child to move in his world with the ease and the grace of President Kennedy, for we know the inner ease, the increased effectiveness, the vastly enlarged circle of responsive warmth he will move in with such an approach. Yet we virtually destroy his chances of doing so by our harping upon his behavioral, postural, physical characteristics, upon his social techniques, even as this was done to us by our parents.

We do not wish to reinforce and to exaggerate a child's natural timidity in a strange situation by calling his painful attention to the outer self—his looks, his speech patterns, his manners. We do wish to strengthen his inner goodness, his responsiveness, his wish to please us, his bottomless reservoir of affection-giving. We do this not by saying, "What a lot of freckles you have!" but by saying, "I loved the nice smile you gave Mrs. Peterson when she complimented you." "I think you're the dearest child in the whole world."

A child's image of himself is based upon his externals, and he is accordingly vulnerable to the infinite number of deviations from some ideal norm that his externals can take. Witness the misery of the early adolescent who varies in appearance a jot from whatever standards are held at the time by his peer group and whose passionate drive toward conformity is usually the despair of his parents.

The self-image of many adults is similarly based upon their external attributes. Witness the frantic search for a youthful appearance among the not-so-youthful and the barrier this search erects against their expanding toward a fulfilling middle and old age. It is not far-fetched to assert that a child is being groomed toward a resistant, resentful, possibly neurotic middle age if his external, rather than his internal, qualities are exclusively commented upon by his parents as he is growing up.

We can now distinguish healthy from painful self-awareness. The former refers to the inner self: "I am warm." "I am interested in others." "*I am good.*" The painfully self-aware person says, "I am too fat." "My head is too round." "I stutter." "I am lazy." "I am selfish." "*I am bad.*"

Identity is essential to happiness for the opposite of all the symptoms of narcissistic identity listed above. Identity means a sense and a feeling of purpose, of mastery over one's feelings and reactions and behavior (and the courage not to have to have mastery over them), of worth and value and importance to others. Above all, identity means a sense of dignity and that, though it is indeed circular defining, means self-respect.

The dignity of a child is necessary to his authenticity. A child is given dignity, and he then experiences its proud and quiet assurance, when he is responded to as an individual, not as a "child" or a "four-year-old" or as an embodiment of his father's faults, or as any kind of representative of some category, usually negative, like "spoiled brat" or "underachiever." If he is put in any of these boxes his dignity as an individual is denied him, and he will resist and rebel. There will be—in his deteriorating self-assurance, his diminishing and diffusing sense of self—a feeling of loss, of emptiness, and of vague but powerful resentment. His behavior will become inappropriate and hostile, either passively or actively. Without at all knowing why, without knowing that the foundations of his self-esteem and dignity are being shaken by his parents' refusal or inability or unwillingness to react to him as an individual, he will begin to develop the corrosive patterns of feeling inferior and inadequate, somehow not quite up to standard, that can haunt him and make a failure of interpersonal and occupational endeavors for the rest of his life.

He is not unlike his parents. We, too, when categorized or "diagnosed" in behavior terms, experience the same sensation of diminished dignity, and we may be permanently shattered by it. There are psychiatrists who believe they are doing their jobs well by telling patients that they are schizophrenic or neurotic or castrating or latently this or that unspeakable thing. The psychiatrists are reinforced in their

behavior by the seductive need of many sick and dependent people to be told just these destructive—and
probably inaccurate—bits of information. But even
the patient who most loudly implores his psychiatrist,
"Tell me what's wrong with me," is going to be deeply
wounded by so ready and cavalier a response to his
neurotic request (a request may be neurotic without
necessarily meaning that the patient is neurotic),
and his deep resentment of the doctor will bring guilt
in its wake at feeling resentful. He will get sicker.
His increased dependence will irritate the doctor,
who will then call him new, more unspeakable names,
and the "therapeutic" relationship will deteriorate
and terminate in unresolved rancor and long-lasting
scars within both patient and doctor.

As with children, so with adults. We are not types;
we are persons seeking identity and meaningfulness,
and we frequently falter and go amiss in the search.
Neither children nor adults are helped back on the
road toward meaningfulness, toward identity, toward
dignity, by being labeled, even by so-called experts.

In helping our children toward dignity, we dignify
ourselves, but it is an interesting phenomenon that
we often fail to recognize this elementary truth until
it is pointed out by our children's behavior, behavior
designed to help *us* toward dignity. A young man,
newly married, asks his father, from whom, in a
childish series of mutual recriminations throughout
the years, he has been long estranged, to his new

apartment to meet his new wife. The father arrives, bearing a large sack of groceries. The young man looks at his father, at the gift, and is free enough to be able to say what he feels: "Put the groceries down out there, Dad, and *you* come in. We just want you." The father cannot make so honest, so simple, so authentic a declaration, but following his son's lead he soon becomes able to speak just as genuinely of his own feelings. The long, wasted, stupid years of alienation end in an evening.

It may be that we have to take the initial cue for dignified behavior from our dignified babies and children and adolescents, for we may have lost our own capacity to act with dignity somewhere along the way through the years. Our rages, our bouts of self-pity, our phoninesses, our acts of pettiness and cruelty, the many ways in which we have tried to lower, to dehumanize, to debase, and to degrade ourselves—these have all led to our loss of dignity and self-respect. We could do far worse, in seeking a model to emulate—to bring back pride, to ennoble us—than to look into the clear, unflinching eyes of our youngsters. Children have a natural dignity so impressive that it seems almost deliberately vicious for an adult to damage it with humiliation, punishment, ignoring, talking down to, etc. The unshifting gaze of the eighteen-month-old; the firm-jawed (but trembling-lipped) standing up of the nine-year-old for her rights; the heartbreaking beauty of a twelve-year-old's brave apologies to the irate old woman on his paper route; the quiet, clear-eyed strength of an adolescent as he watches his drunken father stumble home. These youngsters tower above us, in our inconsistent sloppiness, our narcissism, our abandonment of self-respect. We can well envy them their youthful dignity. It is a pity that we often feel we have to deprive them of it, by whatever undignified, and numerous, means at our disposal. It is the more admirable that they are able to maintain their dignity in the face of our onslaughts against it.

A professional therapist will not be needed if we respect our children; if we acknowledge, admire, and do not despoil their dignity; if, in short, we allow them normal and unfettered identity-formation. They will be firm of purpose, spontaneous in expression, and genuine in giving affection. They will be happy, and so will we.

VIII:
The Pathologies

I only hope that when I am free
As they are free to go in quest
Of the knowledge beyond the bounds of life
It may not seem better to me to rest.

—Robert Frost, "Misgiving"

Some children are not free, and it does seem better to them to rest. They are called "underachievers," for one thing—"spoiled" or "emotionally disturbed" or "delinquent" or "bad" for several other things.

If, however, we are really to understand our unfree children, those with the symptoms of real pathology, then we must learn to stop thinking of them in terms of labels and to allow our understanding to sift down to levels of feeling-with them. Compassion, empathy, parental love are what are needed, not psychiatric terminology and especially not the terminology of hostility, which is well represented by the terms "spoiled," "bad," and "delinquent." It is a defensible hypothesis that the hostility of adults, expressed in this unfightable name-calling, is itself responsible for the conditions of the children whom they so gleefully and destructively label. As long as we set up our children—as our enemies—as long as we begrudge their intrusions upon our lives, our quiet, our interest; as long as we resent their reminding us of our responsibilities—for so long are we going to have to deal somehow with unhappy and unfree children. If we deal with them by name-calling and punishment we are increasing their unhappiness and their bondage, and we are going to become still more angry, begrudging, and resentful of them. The circle expands wickedly, and we finally have to call for professional help.

Professional help does not always work for all. It works a little. There is the "application phenomenon" (or the "telephone cure") which describes the "miraculous" improvement of the disturbed child in the interval between the parent's call to the clinic or to the child therapist and the first appointment. There is the cathartic and overwhelming relief, once in the therapist's office, of having an intelligent, non-judgmental, and reasonably quiet listener. For the child, there is the similar relief of seeing a reasonably non-bromidic, non-moralistic adult who is as open to liking him as not. This leads to a temporary abeyance of anxiety and symptoms in adult and child. There is the "transference cure," in which the sheer joy of building rapidly, from scratch, a meaningful relationship with another human being temporarily pushes discomfort and pain to the background. Needs to be taken care of are satisfied, for adults and children alike—which is more deeply gratifying to everyone than he'd care to admit: "My worries, my troubles are now in the hands of someone who knows more about living than I do. I am, finally, safe."

And there is the solid, gradual, incremental building up of self-confidence, of self-respect, of self-expression, of decision-making, and of creativity that, directed by a conscientious and gifted therapist over a long period of time and at the considerable expenses of emotional drainage, constant self-doubting and self-questioning on the part of both patient and therapist, is the closest known thing to a cure.

Professional help does not always work because, simply, it is too little and too late to combat the years of punishment and name-calling that have become so integral a part of the parent-child relationship that they keep popping up at times of stress or lack of control, in spite of the firmest resolves against them. "The doctor says I have to love the little bastard" is a statement far more telling than the doctor's advice, and it is far more indicative of the future of the relationship. So again, for real change, through stressful as through tranquil times, the feeling-with the child is essential, far more so than the transitory advice of the doctor, rational "understanding" of the child, or, all too often, psychotherapy.

We cannot feel-with a child if we are hostile toward or resentful of him. All we can do is call him names, or complain about him to anyone who will listen. In this name-calling and complaining we reveal our own problems—our weak points, our intolerances, our deficiencies in understanding—to anyone who will listen and think a little. Custom dictates that we agree with the point of view espoused by the person talking to us. This is called "making friends and influencing people," and it is unfortunately thought to be more important than letting our real reactions be known, which might alienate people. The result is that we can always find support for our complaints about our children, even from doctors, and most certainly from the pharmacist and the schoolteacher and the lady next door, all of whom have some investment in remaining "friends" with us. The shame of institutionalized education is that professionals—teachers and principals—have willingly allowed lay people—parents and boards of education—to dictate policy to them. This is as incredible a self-deprofessionalization as it would be if physicians or lawyers or any other professional group were to similarly allow themselves and their professional activities to be governed by nonprofessionals.

We do not witness the unspoken disagreement, the disgust—voiced after we have left our "friends" —with our self-pitying and ignorant complaints. If we are lucky, we have perhaps one friend who does speak her mind, who is secure enough not to have to placate and agree with us. If we recognize ourselves as lucky to have such a friend, we are even luckier, for the usual tendency is to break off relations at once with so unfeeling a boor. If we *really* want to make friends and influence people, we will never hesitate in voicing our opinions, no matter how unpopular, for the people we like the most will respect us for it and want to develop the friendship. She, and most of the inarticulate others, see through the complaints to the self-pity beneath, but our familiar defense of not granting others our own sensitivities keeps us from knowing we are revealed, and we continue calling our children names.

We also feed their pathology, for it is impossible, even for the sturdiest child, to answer the charge that he is spoiled, or lazy, or no good. "I am *not*" is a response not likely to be honored, he well knows, but he is not sophisticated enough, nor brave enough, nor impractical enough to engage his parents in a discussion of semantics. His parents know this full well, by the way, and their smug utilization of such advantage against the child is yet another ring in the expanding circles of his resentment.

The authentic parent knows his hostility for what it is and accordingly takes it upon himself, dealing with it howsoever he is able. He does not take it out on his child or on anyone else. If the husband has come to feel contempt for his wife or hatred of the bondage he sees his marriage as having become; if she has come to bridle at having been cast as mother, or daughter, when she wants to be a wife; if either the husband or wife has, or thinks he or she has, out-grown the other; if the previously latent pathology of the other has grown more and more overt through the years—from excessive neatness to "perfection-ism," from excessive social drinking to alcoholism; if sexual hang-ups, perversions, inhibitions, unmarked in the intensity of youthful ardor, now with the rapidly declining libido of the sexually maladjusted show up, with resulting frustrations and mounting tensions—if any (or, God forbid, all) of these famil-iar marital problems are eating away at the authentic parent, even then he can take them upon himself and try to figure out what, if anything, to do about them. Authentic people can have serious problems, but they do not project them onto other people. They especially do not project them onto their children.

For this reason, and because of his genuine love and respect for the child, the authentic parent does not have disturbed children. His children are noisy and quarrelsome and contentious and competitive and thoughtless and forgetful and clumsy. They are generous and affectionate and witty and stoical and cooperative. They affect repellently phony manner-isms, and they pierce the phoniness of others. They bear themselves with dignity and grace, and they forgive—always, and again and again they forgive—the loss of dignity in others.

The authentic parent appreciates the complexities, the side-by-side contradictions, of his children, and

with humor and grace and awe watches the unfold-
ing of these myriad traits. He speaks with pride, not
with a whine, about his children, but his greatest joy
in them is inward and quiet. There is an unspoken
richness of feeling within this parent as he watches
or plays with or talks to his children, and it gives him
pleasure to know that he would never leave them. He
will let them, easily, leave him, but he knows that if
he can help it nothing short of death will remove him
permanently from this unequaled source of richness.

The children of the inauthentic parent are unhappily different. They are the spoiled, the bad, the
phobic, the fantasy-dwellers, the decompensated, the
underachieving, the neurotic children. They are the
arsonists, the transvestites, the delinquents, the ex-
hibitionists and voyeurs. They are the sufferers—
from bedwetting and soiling, asthma, anxiety, depression. They are excessively rivalrous, excessively
achieving, excessively polite, excessively "good." They
are hypochondriacs and glue sniffers and pot blowers.
They lie and they steal, and they fear the truth. The
boys become sadistic, the girls become pregnant.

Can we feel with these children, and in so doing
help them on the road toward authenticity? We must.
There is no other way if they are to be helped. And
they must be helped.

Consider Robert, a "spoiled" child, according to the
unanimous testimony of his grandparents, teachers,
neighbors, and father. His mother is more inclined

to diagnose Robert as "misunderstood," and she has, faithful to her diagnosis, alienated Robert's teachers, neighbors, her parents, and her husband. They, in turn, lose no time in labeling her a neurotic mother, which justifies their irritation with her. Her husband has long since stopped talking to her on any level but that of immediate practicalities. She senses easily the barely disguised groans and eyes rolled heavenward every time she goes to Robert's school. The principal, self-righteous in his weary knowledge of her neuroticism, automatically discounts anything she says, which she well knows, and he has officially told Robert's teacher to do the same. Robert's mother feels increasingly that she is in a smoky Kafka-esque void, her weakening cries that her son be given attention yielding only discordant echoes. She continues crying, though, and her martyrdom is becoming almost sensually gratifying to her as she fights the heroic fight against the unbeatable foe for the sake of her son.

Robert is eleven and obese. He is a bully, and he is loud and unpleasant. Once in an unguarded moment, he said his only wish was that all the kids at school consider him their best friend. His behavior, however, in complete opposition to his fantasy, is unendingly designed to bug, to torture, to alienate all the kids at school. His laugh is raucous and cruel. His hands are forever poking and pinching, hurtfully and obscenely, the other children. He greets adults with a shattering blow to their shoulders. Nobody (including his mother) likes him.

Robert's therapist (who doesn't like him, either), massaging his aching shoulder, dictates, following a session with the boy: "The closer I get to verbalizing with Robert his feeling of despair and loneliness, the stronger his resistance becomes, the more deafening his laugh, designed to drown out my words, the more assaultive his physical relationship with me. His scorn at the 'sissy' and 'baby' toys and games in the playroom, his ear-shattering scrambling techniques at any attempts at verbal communication seem virtually impenetrable. Robert is not the only one in the playroom who despairs."

Robert's strength and ferocity, his unpleasant forcefulness that subdues and drowns out all opposition, have created a world of perfect freedom for him, over which he reigns by terror, a lonely tyrant, striking out at the enemies on his borders. His mother and his therapist are simply spies, filtering through the borders, infringing upon his dreadful freedom. But Robert is not truly free. He is trapped, by his cumulative rejections, within his bristling fortress and he cannot get out any more than others can get in.

Robert can get out if he chooses to, but he can choose only if he is truly free. As long as he must fortify himself against rejection, and as long as he must fight fire with fire (and he sees fire even when, rarely, it does not exist), he is still in bondage, and his behavior will eventuate in expulsion from school and from his family and, not unbelievably, in ultimate membership in the Hell's Angels.

Robert got out of his fortified prison with the help of a college boy whom the therapist, claiming failure on his own part, finally recommended to Robert's mother. This young man, a football player, had been like Robert when he was younger, but had had the good fortune of having an involved father, a farmer, who refused to see his boy destroy himself, and who took his rehabilitation firmly in hand. The student met Robert three afternoons a week (at $1.50 an hour, compared with the therapist's $30) nominally for tutelage and companionship, actually for liberation. Unthreatened by Robert's violence, unrepulsed by his personality, this young man met Robert's challenge head-on. If Robert wanted to fight, they fought —and Robert lost. If Robert wanted to taunt or to laugh, he was nondefensively, even amusedly, taunted back and outlaughed by the undevious, sincere, and merry young man. Withal, out of the depths of his own security and calm knowledge of his own likability, the college boy never once stopped liking Robert. He got furious at him, he pounded both of Robert's shoulders black and blue, he railed at him, sometimes for an hour at a time. But Robert sensed the boy's regard for him. At first appeared a hero-worshiping reaction that the athletic young man instantly inspired in all preadolescent boys; later, when

Robert had begun to drop some of his defenses, he sensed directly both the boy's warmth and imperturbability. Still later, Robert's positive feelings for the boy were greatly increased by the beginning of a process of identifying with him. He stopped wolfing down food in the gargantuan manner he had long been enjoying, as stuffing for his emotional void; and in an attempt to emulate his companion in his muscular physique he lost weight rapidly. There was no coercion, no shaming, no diet. Robert wanted to look like his hero, and he decided the best way to do it was to lose weight and then to exercise; and so he did freely.

Robert made another decision, equally freely, after a month of the college boy's companionship. He said that he'd like to invite his father on one of their outings. The father, shocked out of his withdrawal by his son's spontaneous invitation, accepted with real gratitude. The three of them thoroughly enjoyed an afternoon baseball game and a dinner out. Robert, in his ecstasy, was almost too well behaved. The father, feeling more and more affection for his son brimming up in him through the day and frankly enjoying the respectful yet light-hearted manner of the likable young man, experienced a new sense of freedom himself. And *he* thereupon began to make decisions, one of which was to take an active part on Robert's side against the smothering ministrations of his wife. Robert's mother, incidentally, reacted to this change in her husband with undisguised relief and delight.

For one thing, it showed her, finally, that someone else did understand Robert and, for another, that someone was reacting to her, even negatively. The mother and father began to talk to each other again.

The beginning of Robert's story is unimportant. It has long been considered important that his therapist understand it, and equally important that the college boy not understand it. The college boy might be biased by knowing the background and react to Robert as a case, not as a boy. The therapist could not make a reliable diagnosis unless he did know the background. But the therapist failed, and the PE major succeeded. To see a child—or a husband or a mother-in-law—as he is at the moment is to see him clearly. The ending of the sad drama of Robert was a happy one, as endings are if they are preceded by the protagonist's and the *dramatis personae*'s chance to make decisions freely.

Ellen was also considered a spoiled child. She was sixteen and might be described as pretty if she did not wholeheartedly and excessively adopt the very most unbecoming styles of hair, make-up, and dress the moment they were introduced. Ellen, to hear her tell her side of the story, had no freedom at all. She had to be home by some arbitrary and unrealistic hour. Her friends and dates were dictated by her step-mother, and she was allowed no choice at all. She had to defer to her father, a dentist, on the use of the tele-phone, to her older sister on the use of the car, and it wasn't fair! Ellen, in her sophomore year in high school, was earning about eighty percent Ds and twenty percent Fs on her report cards. She had an impressive record at Juvenile Hall for petty theft and was, in fact, an accomplished thief. She was gaunt and unhealthy-looking. She had made several LSD trips and blew pot regularly at the frequent parties of her overprivileged friends. She was the class prostitute and boasted of having laid everyone on the football team except the "fairy quarterback." She hated everyone, especially her sister, her stepmother, her father, her teachers, her friends, and in general men and women. She was in love, of course, and had laid careful plans to become pregnant before school was out in June to ensure an immediate wedding and a final termination of schooling.

By almost anyone's standards, the prospects for Ellen were bleak. Yet psychotherapy was successful in her case. Ellen was clearly a pathologically dependent, passive, suggestible child, and she made her choices unfreely, completely on the basis of what she felt the currently significant persons in her life would either applaud or be devastated by. Either effect was worth making a decision for, yet how limited such a decision is, when it can lead to only one effect or, at the most, two!

Ellen was right: she was not free. But while she interpreted her bondage in temporal and physical terms, we see it as the familiar bondage of restricted and predetermined choices. Testing her parents, she chose that which most aggravated them; her peers, that which she thought would most please them. Robert needed and found someone to care. But what if no one cared what Ellen did? Her therapist called Ellen and her parents together for what he may have called, awkwardly, "conjoint" therapy. He knew Ellen's father both socially and professionally (he was a patient of the dentist), and he counted on his friend's basic liberalism, amicability, and openness to suggestion to follow his daughter's lead.

Ellen indeed led the discussion. For several hours, feeling safe in "her" therapist's benignness, she blasted her father and stepmother, blaming him for her real mother's death four years previously, blaming her stepmother for favoring her own children and unjustly making Ellen a Cinderella in the ashes. Throughout, her parents listened attentively, agreeing at times, disagreeing at others, but never denying Ellen's right to her feelings. A little emboldened, Ellen then began to voice her essential dislike of drugs, sex, and Juvenile Hall, as she finally sensed that her parents might not consider her a baby for fearing these things any more than they had considered her a lost wretch for having said earlier the terrible things about them that she did. Now the child, seeing, voicing, and gaining acknowledgment of her ambivalences, could make a free choice. Some of her choices were between two negatives; some were easy because of the clear distinction between a destructive and a constructive course of action; most were double-edged horns of dilemmas, either way having both positive and negative aspects. Her easiest choice was to give up stealing. Almost as easy was giving up drugs and meaningless sex, since she really liked none of these in the first place, and could now say so to herself. She could not and did not abandon her "love" for the boyfriend, and no pressure was put on her to do so. The parents later learned that he was a sensible but frightened kid, who solved the problems that a premature marriage would have created by dropping out of school prior to Ellen's next ovulation period and enlisting in the Navy.

The child who sets fires is acting out a hostile compulsion to destroy, as he feels he has been destroyed, and a perverse need for intense stimulation because he feels ignored and unstimulated himself. He could be acting out a dozen other drives, and only individual study of such a child will tell which they are. But whatever he is expressing, it is determined by those past experiences that have been so intense as to narrow his range of choices in the present: in this case, as narrow as whether or not to strike the match. It is a match, and not a gun or a switchblade, by virtue of its availability and his youth or the television show he saw that afternoon when he should have been in school—all chance factors and therefore unpredictable and inexplicable. If the child had not been ignored and unstimulated, he would not have built up so passionate a need for stimulation as could be satisfied only by a conflagration. If he had not been beaten, he would not have felt the natural reaction to beat back and to destroy. The combination of alternate ignoring and beating is a poisonous one, and it is guaranteed to pay dividends in the form of destroyed property and, possibly, destroyed people. It removes the alternative: the only thing the child can do is to strike the match, and run. If, however, the child is treated with warmth and compassion, and is given attention freely and ungrudgingly, then the alternative—not to strike the match—not only appears, but very likely dominates.

The boy of ten or more whose divorced father rarely sees him, who dresses in his mother's or sister's or female neighbor's underclothes, has made a desperate, a painful choice: he will deny his instincts, his fragmentary identification patterns with men, and he will become a woman, since it is all too clear to him that only femininity is valued or that masculinity is devalued. This is not the boy, it should be stated at once, who ultimately becomes homosexual. There is more than a fifty-fifty chance that he will, to be sure, but it is by no means inevitable at this first stage of transvestism.

If this boy is fortunate enough to get a good stepfather, whose secure masculinity changes his mother's evaluation of men from negative to positive, from castration to admiration, then the chances of his choosing masculinity over femininity are vastly increased. If he can come to think of himself as truly independent of his passive, or absent, or dead father and able to be masculine even with the redoubtable handicap of having a weak model, or none, to emulate, then he can choose, if he wishes, masculinity over femininity. Male homosexuals defend their sexual orientation by saying that they had no choice —that they were always committed to homosexuality, by virtue of their mothers' character and their fathers' lack of it. They may be right, and all the insight or therapy or endocrinology in the world may well be too late to alter the consequences of their reaction—a choice that is not a choice—to the deadly pattern of maternal-dominance/paternal-passivity. There are many happily heterosexual men who came from a mother-dominant/father-passive home, and they are the ones who had a choice—whose parents, transcending their own personal and sexual problems, were able to give their sons enough freedom, who were mature enough not to have to burden these little boys with the crippling weight of their own anxieties. They did not enlist the boys as either scapegoats or confidants, and the boys remained accordingly free to develop as they wished.

The tendency to make sweeping generalizations, such as "Dominant mothers produce effeminate sons," ignoring the many dominant mothers who give their sons freedom of choice, is an unfortunate symptom of our psychological times. It is appropriate and praiseworthy to attempt to induce generalizations from observation and experimentation, but we are not justified in deducing conclusions from the generalizations to apply to specific cases. Barrett says: "This capacity for living easily and familiarly at an extraordinary level of abstraction is the source of modern man's power. . . . But it is also a power which has, like everything human, its negative side, in the desolating sense of rootlessness, vacuity, and the *lack of concrete feeling* that assails modern man in his moments of real anxiety." (Italics are mine.)

Elsewhere, he states, ". . . every effort at understanding must take off from our actual situation, the point at which we stand." It is at this point, considering concretely the individual child in the unique situation, that we must start from in understanding the transvesite boy or the fire-setting boy or Ellen or Robert. A good beginning is to analyze, as well as an outsider ever can, the choices that the child is making: which of them are genuine, free choices, and which of them are reactions to pressure. Even loving parents are very much outsiders, considering the wealth of fantasy, of conceptions and misconceptions, the tangled and alogical—by parental standards—threads of thoughts and ideas in their child of which they are never aware.

It is safe to say that a symptom, or behavior, that is

usually of concern to parents and always of concern to the child is a reaction to some unhealthy, limiting force or situation. A decision, made alone or after real communication with someone, whether wise or injudicious, is a choice. It is worthy of praise and respect. A child who makes choices instead of developing symptoms is growing up. Choice-making, like symptom-formation, is learned. It improves and becomes more efficient with practice, and it is encouraged to develop by rewards when it is displayed. Rewards are psychologically meaningful reinforcements. They do not include bribes, such as money or a new Jaguar, and they are not to be "understood" by the child, as in the case where the parent says, "If he's bad, I let him know it. If I don't say anything, then he understands he's doing all right." They include praise, and hugging and kissing, and the clear thrill of sparkling eyes and a smile directed at the child, the look that glows within the child for years and years afterward.

Children who make choices grow into adults who make choices. These are the adults who are on top of their world, who take active steps in the management of their lives and for whom, therefore, life is lived as they wish it to be lived. It is right for them. They are the happy ones, the authentic, the actualized ones. We can wish no greater fortune for our children.

IX:

The Contingencies

Divorce is a solution to a problem. It is often a wise solution; it is often a very poor solution, reflecting immaturity, lack of emotional control, lack of insight, and lack of patience on the part of one or both of the partners. It is always bad on children. It is devastating and disrupting, and it makes them doubt themselves and feel guilty. It creates voids in their lives that shouldn't be, and it predisposes them, because they are deprived of the experience of living with people who solve their problems by means other than divorce, to divorce themselves. It retards them, for the entire mystique of divorce is based upon blame, legally reinforced—indeed, insisted upon. The child who early learns that bad situations are someone else's fault is truly retarded in his development of authenticity.

Death is also, sometimes, a solution to a problem. It may be the inevitable solution to a physical condition. It may be the sick and misguided solution, in suicide, to an emotional or social problem. It may, also in suicide, be a dignified solution to an intolerable situation. It is often, more often, not a solution: the shocking, unbelievably sudden outcome of an accident; the senseless, wasteful victimization of murder or war. It is always bad on survivors, and it is particularly bad on surviving children. It is agonizing and rupturing. It creates a void that should not be. It makes children feel guilty and painfully responsible. It utterly eliminates, of course, any possibility of working things out with the dead person, of communicating with him, of increasing mutual understanding with him. It is a hideous lesson in the unpredictability of life and affairs; it is an awful look into the chasm of devastating uncertainty. It leads to fears, phobias, nightmares. It creates a ferment of a sense of loss and a consequent search for restitution that may last for years, or forever.

Like divorce, death occurs in the experience of children. Even if divorce and death don't happen, children fear that they might. "Contingency means that what will become actual is contingent upon many influences, many variables, so many that they may well be infinite in number. The fact of contingency means that I never can predict with complete assurance. The experience of contingency means that I live with anxiety."*

Children, like adults, must live with contingency.

* J. F. Bugental, *Challenges of Humanistic Psychology* (New York: McGraw-Hill, 1967), p. 22.

They are given little choice, to be sure, in the endless parental admonitions such as "Don't do that; you'll get hurt," but this is neurotic contingency, not the existentially unavoidable contingencies of death, guilt, and anxiety, and the statistically unavoidable contingency of divorce. To be forever reminding a child of possible harmful consequences of his behavior is to be setting the stage for the early development of fears, phobias, hesitancies, self-doubts. It contributes to motor awkwardness because of the motor conflicts involved, as between climbing and not climbing, leaping and walking sedately. It sometimes contributes, because of the generalized inhibition of virtually any locomotion—"to move, especially to move fast, is to get hurt"—to obesity. It teaches not caution but immobilization. It adds to the increasing feminization of boys and to the shrill fearfulness of girls, both of which are unbearably irritating to parents, who thereupon add to the complex they abhor by repeating, louder, their warnings and injunctions.

By now, *mutatis mutandis*, the fearful child has become the fearful adolescent, so the parents adapt to the change appropriately by warning of the now more painful social consequences: "Nobody's going to like you if you keep acting like that." "Nobody loves a sissy . . . a fatty . . . a crybaby."

Children do not always break their legs or get burned when they venture out of protective inhibition, but they do experience guilt and anxiety. The guilt and anxiety stem from breaking through the protective inhibitions which the young person must do—as he knows deeply, inarticulately, within himself—if he is to develop freely. But he wishes, also deeply and inarticulately, and much more strongly than his "protective" parents know, to remain within the boundaries they set. He wants to please them, he wants not to cause them anxiety, and besides, he's a little scared himself.

When he is away from home, and the prescribed curfew time is approaching, perhaps has passed already, the child, regardless of the extent to which he pretends not to care, begins to experience the guilt that, as he says, ruins his evening. There are many reactions to this guilt, and none of them is healthy. He may strengthen his façade of not caring into overt defiance. He may figure he might as well act out whatever fears for his behavior his parents have expressed, as long as he's probably going to be accused of, and punished for, them anyhow. He may fashion for himself a premature independence while still needing his parents' concern and advice. He may develop a coldness, an unreachability, a closing of the gates of communication between him and his parents. And always, underlying his reaction, whatever it may be, is the sick feeling, Mom's awake, pacing the floor, and when I get home she's going to yell and scream and cry, and I've got to just stand there and take it. His evening or his afternoon, in the case of a younger child, is ruined, and whatever opportunities for unpressured fun, for growth, for real independence that may still be open are lost, turned into possibly inappropriate, perhaps even dangerous actings-out of his guilt and anxiety.

This is not to say that parents should not impose curfews, set expected times for children to come home. These are necessary and appropriate, and they furnish the child with the secure structure of knowing his parents care for him. Just listen to the ill-hidden pride in a young girl's voice as she announces that if she doesn't get right home her father will "kill" her. She loves saying this and is happy that she can say it.

But curfews become restrictive and lead to inauthentic behavior on both child's and parent's parts if they are imposed out of mistrust and anxiety, if they are based upon attempts to outwit the contingencies and thereby artificially load the child with fears, or if they are symptomatic of the parental overprotection that inhibits a child's free development.

Children will, of course, ultimately die, as will their parents earlier. The existential realities can and should be acknowledged by the parents as sources of a child's unhappiness. If even this acknowledgment becomes repetitious or compulsive, or if it is used as a means to control and manipulate a child, it loses its force as a comforting and compassionate support to what the child already knows but may not be able to speak of, thereby suffering from its unspeakableness. The contingencies can and should, when the child is caught in the dread of their possible actualization, be similarly acknowledged. "Yes, Mama could have been in an accident. But I'm not worried. She's a good driver, and she's never been in one yet, and I believe in going on the past record instead of worrying."

"If Daddy and I do get divorced, dear—and it looks like we will—it will just be because we'll both be happier by living away from each other. We want to be happy just as we want you to be happy, and this way seems the best to us."

If the conversation with the child is not to control but to clarify, not to burden but to enlighten, then it will help the child and it will bring him closer to his parent. It will give him a basic strength to deal with the many contingencies that he will face, and he will thank his parents with the heartfelt gratitude that is never felt by the children of neurotic, exploitative, fear-engendering parents. These unhappy children, usually neurotic themselves, become adults who are still bound to their parents. The bonds of resentment are stifling; the bonds of love are liberating.

Evasions trouble a child far more than frank discussions of the crisis at hand that has to be coped with. If the child understands as much as he is capable of, he can choose, out of his unappreciated but extensive reservoir of reactions, those which will be more appropriate, more comforting than not. Prince Hamlet, an early existentialist, said,

> ... for madness would not err,
> Nor sense to ecstasy was ne'er so thrall'd
> But it reserv'd some quantity of choice
> To serve in such a difference. ...
>
> —*Hamlet,* III, 4

If the child does not understand, and if he faces the crisis with vague or explicit feelings of his own responsibility for the situation ("Daddy left because he couldn't stand me crying all night"; "Mamma always said I'd be the death of her, and I was"), then he reacts, and out of his extensive reservoir of defense mechanisms erects those defenses that have served him earlier, in protecting him against the frightening anxiety, to limit him, and to keep him from growing authentically. Such a child is ill-equipped to face future contingencies: he will either search, conflictingly and clashingly, for certainties that don't exist, or he will refine and elaborate his techniques of defense against anxiety to the point of a full-fledged neurosis.

It is far easier, far kinder, to acknowledge and to allow the expression of a child's confusion, grief, and self-recriminations. It is strengthening to the child to have the parent acknowledge and express his own confusion, grief, and self-recriminations in his presence. Children fall apart much less easily than we might think; but if they do, it is only when the adults around them fall apart. We are strengthened ourselves, in adversity, by the expression of our tumult and are therefore that much less likely to show the child complete helplessness and lack of control.

A father returned to work on the afternoon of the funeral of his much-loved son, killed shockingly and tragically. He let it be known that he wanted no mention made of his loss, and his colleagues and employees respected his wishes, though they felt it was wrong not to be able even to voice their sympathy. In later months, to his psychiatrist, whom the father had had to consult for symptoms of suicidal depression, he said, "If only I'd let the heartbreak come out when Pete was killed. Where do we get this phony, dangerous idea of trying to fool ourselves and everyone else into thinking we're not human, not grieving, not weeping in every cell?"

Death, deformity, divorce, displacement can happen, and there is no good defense against any of them. There are only neurotic defenses, which are not defenses because they lower our tolerance for the next contingency. Wars and riots and automobile accidents happen, and once caught in their frenzy, we with difficulty avoid being swept along to their violent conclusions. We cannot predict or escape contingency, but we, and our children, in the very knowledge of it, will find ourselves coping with it without being paralyzed by fear.

In this day of multiple divorces and households consisting of "his, hers, and their" children, the perplexity of relationships between stepparents and stepchildren and among half-siblings and step-siblings represents a contingency that usually *is* predictable: it will be a mess. For it is every bit as difficult to predict one's future relationship with one's new wife's children—especially those from her next-to-last marriage!—as it was as a young bridegroom to predict the kind of father to one's own children one might become. Indeed, it is more difficult, for many reasons, the chief one being the presence, in a stepparent-stepchild relationship, of a host of unconscious, or at least unstated and suppressed, attitudes on the part of both stepparent and stepchild toward the other. The off-stage but vivid presence of the stepchild's natural parent and grandparents adds a constant note of potential strife or threat. The quite natural resentments of many children directed against their stepparents, and the presumably also "natural" resentment of the second or third mate directed against the first or second, or both, add more to the potential explosiveness of the relationship. The inevitable differences in values, child-rearing practices, and other factors, reflected in the home by children of differing backgrounds, play their part. The stepfather's feelings about the natural father, the stepmother's feelings about the natural mother, most of which are probably negative, are often paralleled in their feelings about their stepchildren.

"Nancy's first husband really gave her a bad time, and I've always hated the bastard for what he did to her. I don't think she quite trusts me, even now, and I'll never forgive him for that. So when I began seeing his son mistreating and bullying our little girl, being his father all over again, I saw red! I blistered his bottom until he couldn't sit down for a week. And I kept it up, too, kept up a regular vendetta against the kid, punishing him for being his father's son. If any other kid had done the same thing, I'd have handled it a lot differently. A lot more gently, and a lot smarter. It took me a long time to see—or rather, it took Nancy a long time to *show* me—that he *was* just a kid, and not his father. We're getting on better now, and he doesn't have to bully his sister."

The inescapable fact that children of divorce are almost bound to be disturbed in one way or another, to a greater or lesser degree, also adds, of course, to the adjustment problems in their new home. They may well seem abrasive, contentious; they almost certainly will be testing their own parent and the new parent, and the chips on their shoulders will be all too visible, all too available for a disastrous knocking off.

And still another factor must be considered and

evaluated for its relevance in the new situation: the psychology of the stepparent. What prompts a man or a woman to assume the responsibilities and the seemingly inevitable problems of a ready-made family? Has he not—for presumably he is also a divorcé—already experienced the strife, the competitiveness, the erosion of personal dignity and the death of personal pride, the sexual indignities, and the lack of honesty, of compassion, of intimacy, passion, and communication that bespeak the troubled, the unsuccessful marriage? And if he is not a divorcé but is marrying for the first time, what are the dynamics, the factors involved in his marrying a family instead of a woman?

Now there well may be, of course, no "dynamics" at all, in the slightly ominous sense of the word that makes people hesitate to speak out before the forbidding psychologist who, they feel, looks at his world through spectacles tinted with an ever-present stain of psychopathology. The second marriage, in other words, may be undertaken simply because the two people love each other. Yet it would be less than realistic to be content in every case, especially one's own, with an explanation that could be an overly simplified one. (This caution applies to first marriages, too, and, judging from the statistics on divorce and marital unhappiness, should be applied considerably more often than it is.)

The sadder but wiser comments of two-time losers may illuminate some of the darker dynamics underlying the second marriage:

"It was bad enough when Hal told me he was in love with that woman. And it was hell when he left and practically moved in with her. But when they got married the minute our divorce was final, I don't think I've ever been so depressed. I felt absolutely worthless, a complete failure. My friends' sympathy didn't help, either. It made it worse, in fact, because it seemed somehow to underline how pathetic and abandoned and washed-up I was. So when Mark came along and then proposed, I snapped him up so fast it was indecent. And all because I had to show Hal and everyone else that I *wasn't* washed-up, that I could still attract a man.

"Well, let me tell you, that's no basis for a marriage. And now Mark's the one who's suffering and depressed. God! What a fool I am!"

"I married Marie out of my own weakness and insecurity. I never thought I could even *have* children, much less be a father to them, since I'd always been so convinced of my inferiority, so convinced I could never be a man among men. And I even had this fantasy that if I ever did have children—and I wanted to, wanted to very much, too much, maybe—that they'd be—oh, I don't know. Deformed, maybe, or

retarded, or just weak. Like me. So when I met Marie
and her kids—beautiful, bright, nice children—I
thought more about having them as *my* children than
I did about having Marie as my wife. That's terrible,
isn't it? But I honestly did. So it's no wonder Marie
is leaving me now . . . and she's . . . taking the children
with her."

"I married Eve out of pity, not love. She was so
grateful for anything I did for her after her husband
left her. And the kids—they were so hungry for a
man's attention, they hung on me. And it flattered
me. I saw myself as some great savior of a needy
family. And I thought it was love."

"When Mother married Jim, I hated him. Actually,
that isn't true. He was really nice to Mother, and me,
and if I'd just let my real feelings out, we'd have
been fine. But I guess I thought I *should* hate him.
You know? All the kids at school kept saying how
awful stepfathers are, and everything, and it just
sort of seemed the thing to do to resent him. Kids are
really dumb, aren't they? Anyhow, I was the world's
worst brat. Jim tried for a long time to ignore how
awful I was and to 'understand' and all that. But I
kept it up, knowing I was breaking Mother's heart,
and sort of getting some terrible kick out of it. I was
all—*vengeful* then. I guess a man can take the cold
shoulder and the insults just so long, because he

finally got mean, and started treating Mother badly,
too. And . . . well, you know. He finally left us. It's
all my fault, only I still can't tell Mother I know it
was. I think she's going to get married again, and I'm
going to try to be better this time. But I don't know
if I can. This guy is strictly bad news as far as I'm
concerned . . ."

"Look, I might as well tell it like it was. I *had* to
get married. No, not that. She wasn't pregnant or anything. But I was thirty-five years old, and it was
getting all around that I was queer. The president
gave me the word: get a wife, or get fired. It was as
simple as that. Well, hell, what could I do? Mavis
didn't seem very demanding. She was attractive and
had those great kids. It was a perfect setup for me.
Instant respectability. So I married her. She loved
me, so it worked for a while. But damn it, I'm not
a husband! Ask Mavis. She's not demanding, except
for one thing: she demands a husband. She can't find
one in me, so she's hunting for one somewhere else.
And all I can say is, Good luck, Honey. *Better* luck,
I should say."

These are the voices of hard-earned wisdom speaking of the expensive, wasted, destructive years of
misdirected searching. In some of the voices we hear
the repetitive pattern of drives uninfluenced by experience. We know they will be repeated, with ac-

cumulating expense and waste and destruction, and we shudder at the all-too-predictable outcome: recurrent, endless unhappiness and goals unreached. In some of the voices we hear the beginnings of insight, of personal responsibility, and in them the possibility of fulfillment, of meaningful unions attained and consummated. These are the voices of people beginning to see the truth in themselves, beginning to *be* themselves.

It is not easy to be oneself. The prattling Polonius bids his son, "To thine own self be true," and Laertes loves him for it. With his propensity for the pat phrase, Polonius might have continued: "Know thyself. Express thyself. Fulfill thyself." He would have been right, for we have recognized the truth in his words. Yet we also recognize their emptiness, as we recognize the emptiness of most noble phrases: they express a goal, sometimes beautifully, but they do not describe the route, much less the steps, toward that goal. *We* have to take the steps; we are the searchers, the questers; and each of us has to find his own unique way of stepping toward truth with himself. The search for authenticity is an intensely individual search, and there is no one whose steps we can follow.

Knowing, expressing, fulfilling oneself are the major steps toward truth with oneself. They happen to everyone, but rarely, in those "peak moments" of which Maslow speaks. When they do happen, the life they illuminate and give profound meaning to is richly authentic; and the hope of more such moments is essentially what keeps us going. Why keep on living? Not really for money or status, but in the hope of another experience of joy, of truth with oneself, of completely being oneself.

"I'm most myself when I'm skiing, alone, and every cell in my body seems to tingle with life, and the world around me—the snow, the trees—is so inexpressibly beautiful."

"I'm most myself when I'm with Marge, because I trust her completely, and I never have to play games or assume roles or put up defenses when she's there."

"I'm most myself at work, I'd say. It's so damned important, what I do. And I do it damned well. Sometimes my excitement builds up until I almost choke, and I pour ideas out in a fever, and I never want to stop."

"I'm most myself when I take the children to the park. I just sit back and watch them play, or I read, and I feel so wonderfully fulfilled, loving what I'm doing, loving them. It's crazy, but there always seems to be sunshine around us out there, like a spotlight, no matter what the weather's like."

"I'm most myself right now, talking to you. And at twelve, when I'm meeting Scott for lunch, I'll be most myself then. And later, when I pick Lynne up at school, I'll be most myself then, too. I live for these marvelous moments of contact with people. God, I'm lucky to know so many!"

Some people can sense the truth of themselves, and then act upon it, authentically, only in the presence of others, for it is in others' reactions to them that they test and define themselves. Others can do it only alone, without the distraction, the noise, of incoming and outgoing messages to other people. Some are most in tune with themselves in their fantasies, some in a temple or a church, some outdoors, some in the charged excitement of busy and challenging work. Most, probably, can find illumination to some degree in all of these circumstances, and in the rich diversity of opportunity they can find their truths more wholly.

But whatever the circumstances and wherever the opportunities, the seeker of truth in himself must approach his quest with joy. Truth is not found in depression, and the conclusions reached after self-laceration and self-punishment—"I shall kill myself," "I shall get a divorce"—are invalid conclusions; a reassessment of them at another happier time, even the next day, will at once reveal their shortcomings,

their tragic and unnecessary finality. It is enough of
a job, when depressed, simply to hold oneself together, to refrain somehow from hurtful action. It is
far too much to expect wisdom, even appropriateness,
in any decision based upon so melancholy a state.

If the many moments of joy, the peak moments,
that we can so easily experience in so many situations
seem more concentrated, more frequent at some
times than at others, then a decision based upon this
finding is much more apt to be a wise decision, for it is
based upon the truth of joy. There is no more valid
truth, in spite of our old teachings that say truth
comes from suffering and adversity.

"When I finally took a look at myself and realized
I was truly happy when Lloyd was away on business,
and that I clammed up and really got tense and
frightened when he was home, I knew then that I
had to get a divorce. And I've never regretted it.
Neither has Lloyd."

Let us now listen to some of the voices that speak
of successful second alliances, for these are the
voices of strength, of transcendence over "inevitable"
problems. These are the authentic utterances of
honest people, and their echoes ring bravely in those
whom they address. Hearing them, we can glimpse
the summits of human possibility, the heights and
the depths of problem-solution that can be reached

by any of us, by all of us, if we but allow ourselves to be ourselves.

Martha and Peggy are sisters, pretty and popular girls of nineteen and seventeen, living with their mother and stepfather and leading a busy life of working and studying, dating and playing, giving much of themselves and taking in much of friendship and affection. They thoroughly enjoy their lives, and their enjoyment is infectious. Their friends and their parents' friends take delight in the girls, and their parents do no less. There is much joy in the home. Communication is always there, sometimes deep and intimate, often affectionately ribald, almost always with lighthearted humor.

The girls are on good terms with their natural father and his wife and visit them in another state almost every summer. But their feelings for their new stepfather, whom their mother married only five years ago, are more nearly, if unconsciously, those of children for their real fathers. For Roger, their stepfather, has become their father, and this is a matter of quite conscious knowledge to all of them. Roger is, first of all, a man of warmth and affection: for women, for children and young people, and for his friends, who feel particularly valued—such is the force of Roger's warmth—in being his friend. An exceptionally good athlete in his college days and after as a professional ballplayer, Roger is secure and delighted in his masculinity, and he feels no need for recourse to bullying, coldness, or domineering to prove it. A naturally dominant man, he offers his new family the immense security of someone who knows what he is about and is proceeding to do it, all the time with respect for his own ways and for the ways of others.

Roger is not a paragon, and his wife and step-daughters have many occasions to bemoan some of his ways, as he does with theirs. But none of them has ever regretted his being there. "Roger can be such a fussbudget," Martha says. "I swear, he'd be happier with a family of *slaves*. He can't even stand the kitchen to be messed up when we're *cooking!* But it's O.K. I guess it's good training for Peggy and me. And he is funny about it. He doesn't mind helping us with the dishes, either, although he doesn't have to. In fact, we wish he wouldn't. He works hard for us, and he should be able to relax after dinner. So I guess it's his problem. My psych professor would probably say that Roger is obsessive-compulsive, but I think he's just got this terrific sense of pride in our home, and in us, and in himself. He's sure made me feel proud of everything since I got to know him."

The reality of being a parent, whether biological, adoptive, foster, or "step," lies in the ability to trans-mit a sense of pride to one's children. "Help your children come to like themselves" is the way it's often put in magazine articles, and though it's perhaps easier to understand being proud of oneself than liking oneself, it means essentially the same thing. It is easy for an embittered or a hostile person to destroy a child's pride in himself. Indeed, it sometimes seems as if many parents set out deliberately to do just this, with their unending programs of belittling, debasing, and humiliating their children. But it is fortunately just as easy to build self-pride in a child—if one is secure within oneself first. It involves praise and pleasure in the child and his activities, a communication of liking for the child and respect for the child's importance.

Peggy chimes in. "You know, Roger *always,* and I really mean always, let Martha and me know how important we were to him. It wasn't just Mother he tried to please when they first started going out, although she came first. But we weren't far behind. He always asked us if we'd like to go with them, and what we'd like to do. I know better now, but when our real father left, I always sort of thought it was because we weren't very important to him. Well, when it comes to that, I guess we weren't. Not as important as other things, anyhow. And I think it left a kind of wound that never really healed. Until Roger. He let us know in all kinds of ways—laughing at us and teasing us, and getting us things, and listening to us —that we really were important."

Roger enters, announcing that the girls' rooms are messes and that they're to get in them and start cleaning right now. They wink, whisper, "See?" and disappear. He looks fondly after them. "They're great girls. I always wanted kids. One of the worst things about my first marriage was that Dorothy didn't want any. She was afraid to have children, actually. She could never admit it, but I know she felt she'd treat her children the same way her folks treated her, and the idea completely revolted and scared her. She couldn't bring herself to put herself to the test, and she hated herself for it.

"But I did want kids, badly. I'd had just the opposite kind of childhood. It was great, really beautiful. And I wanted . . . oh, to relive it, I guess, a little, in my own kids. And to give to them everything Mother and Dad gave to me. Sort of a gift of thanks to them, if you'll pardon the corniness. But I was—I am—deeply grateful to them for the happy childhood they gave me. I couldn't thank them a better way than by giving them happy grandchildren. And besides, I just plain *like* kids. They're real, and honest, and funny. They make me feel good, just watching them.

"Well, it didn't work out. Dorothy got to hating herself so much, she began hating me, too. And we broke up. It was pretty rough, and I decided I wouldn't marry again. I was teaching and coaching, and those kids became my kids. It wasn't the real thing, and I didn't try to fool myself that it was, but it wasn't bad. Hell, most people settle for a compromise, and I wasn't any different from or better than anyone else.

So I was doing O.K. Half a life, like so many others, but a good half. And it was a lot better than a bad marriage.

"But then I met Ruth and fell in love with her. I was thirty-eight, a confirmed bachelor, and all I wanted to do was marry her and become whole again. And it was unbelievable, those girls of hers. Wonderful, happy girls. I loved them, too, practically immediately. They were everything I'd ever wanted in children, and I loved Ruth all the more for making such great persons out of them, what with everything she'd been through."

There is a quality in authentic people that may be described as "being there."* It is a kind of solidity; they can be counted on—to listen, to accept, to help. They are reassuring people, and they are important people. They are "there" because they like and are interested in others; the others know it and also become "there." Thus, a permanence and a basicness of relationships can be established in which grievances and conflicts rarely develop beyond a petty and quickly forgotten stage. We need our parents to be there when we need them urgently, as in crisis, and when we don't. We hunger for a basic, real relation-

* The concept of "being there" is borrowed from my friend, Carolyn Mathers, a perceptive and unfortunately unpublished (at this writing) essayist. I thank her for allowing me to use her ideas.

ship, and we have to have at least one at any point in our lives. The authentic parent, biological or otherwise, is there to his children; they then are there to him; and the inevitable problems of adjustment that forever arise stay in their place and do not override and cast out love, if it was there at the beginning. Roger is obviously there to his wife and stepdaughters, and they are there to him. It is a safe bet that this marriage, these relationships, will abide and flourish.

Contingency means that we live each moment on the brink of possible disaster, and it means to children and adults alike that anxiety is our constant companion. Humanism means that our love for ourselves and for each other will not attenuate or deny contingency, but that we can, in good faith, cope with it for better or for worse; and that in the coping we become authentic.

X:

Metaphors of Blood

The June 7, 1968, issue of *Life* magazine was delivered to my office on June 6, a few hours after I had learned of Senator Robert Kennedy's death. In this issue, Senator Eugene McCarthy was quoted as saying, after his victory in the Oregon primary election, that Kennedy had been "pretty well bloodied up."

The timing of the quote was unfortunate, to say the least, and I am sure that Senator McCarthy who, like the rest of us, was still seeing the image of the all too literally bloodied head of his late opponent, regrets most fiercely the untimely publication of his remark.

Yet the metaphor is of our time, and even the peaceful McCarthy must assume responsibility for adding to the vocabulary of violence which is so limitlessly and apparently inextricably a part of our language and our reactions. John Chancellor, the NBC reporter, for example, described the many noted persons leaving St. Patrick's Cathedral after Senator Kennedy's funeral as an "arsenal of power." Semanticists have long told us of the power of words, how they structure and shape our deepest reactions. Words are not only symbols, once or twice removed from the realities of love and hate; rather, they stimulate, direct, even create love and hate—and fear and violence. A five-year-old child is not a semanticist, but he wonders despairingly if his mother might not really do it when she threatens, "I'll kill you!" The mother will protest, "He knows I was only *saying* that," but the child, unconvinced that her words were unreal, is far more sophisticated than she: he senses in his mother's threat the real kernel of murderousness lying at its center. When later he suffers the spanking that represents the next stage in his mother's breakdown of control, he appreciates even more convincingly the essential identity of word and deed. He does not understand the psychodynamics of the spanking: the mother's emotional immaturity, her own regular spankings as a child, her predictable inflictions upon someone else of her own frustrations and inadequacies, her interpersonal narrowness that allows of only one means—physical violence—of dealing with a child's recalcitrances. He understands only the important thing: that when his mother says something, she means it—far more than she knows.

In the same issue of *Life*, an article by Donald Jackson titled "Mike Bell Is Waiting" tells of Bell, convicted of shooting and killing Police Officer Carl Knobbe in Denver in September 1962 and still awaiting execution in Death Row, Colorado State Penitentiary (where he seems not especially penitent). Jackson quotes Bell's mother as saying about her son, "His father used to beat him with a folded rope until it scared me. . . . Mike would always get beat on more than the others. But he would never cry, even when he was little. I guess it was satisfying not to let Bell [Mike's alcoholic father] make him cry."

The cries on June 6, 1968, are for *doing* something about the mindless tide of violence in our country— once again surgent in the hideous murder of a good man. Congress rushes through an attenuated firearms control bill, deploring the ungoverned availability of weaponry—except when it brings in revenue. Terrence O'Flaherty, television critic for the San Francisco *Chronicle,* deplores the diet of murder ingested by children all day long on the tube. Anti-Americans deplore the competitive climate of capitalism. The politically astute point to the three evils epitomized by the assassins of President Kennedy, Martin Luther King, Jr., and Robert Kennedy: communist-anarchism, white racism, and destructive chauvinism, respectively. Richard Goodwin, writer and adviser to Senator Kennedy, in an interview with John Chancellor on June 7, 1968, laid the blame, variously, on the Vietnam war, racism, poverty, and smog. He also cited people's feelings of futility, defeatism, and lack of control over their lives.

Mental illness is blamed, the decline in church attendance is blamed, the far Right is blamed, anti-intellectualism is blamed. (May it not be significant that these three men, each noted for his high intelligence, died of bullets in their heads, the seat of intelligence?) Society itself, our eternal scapegoat, has been blamed in its demands, willingly acceded to by many, for conformity. "Commitment!" becomes the rallying cry, the cure for the blind puppetry of people caught in mindless servitude to whatever clichés that currently prevail, most of which are one or another form of repression: ban youth, ban pot, ban sex, ban anything that in any way implies unfettered freedom. Freedom, our "free" society says in its many ways, is dangerous: it must be contained, it must be stamped out, it must be punished. A commitment to freedom, therefore, is urged by the humanist as an antidote to servility, to sterility, to slavery.

The humanist is right. Congress is right, and Terrence O'Flaherty and Richard Goodwin are right, and so are all the others who deplore the infections in the bloodstreams of our lives that show themselves shockingly in the pus of assassinations and battered children and wars.

Yet the solutions proposed by these committed people, these bright, heartsick people, seem empty. They are too superficial, or too vague. They urge upon us attitudes of peace that cannot prevail over our built-in aggressiveness, our murderousness, our heritage of violence. To say to a virulent anti-Semite, Love thy neighbor—to say to a parent routinely beaten up when he was a child, Honor and cherish gently your own child—to say to a Southern bigot, All men are created equal—to say to a violence-obsessed, death-loving, gun-bearing psychopath, Thou shalt not kill —to say all this is to speak unheard and unattended. It is not to the behavior, the bigotry, the brutality, that we must appeal, for they will remain unalterably functions of the underlying hatred, quick to explode in crisis or confrontation—as quickly as five minutes after listening to, and agreeing with, a sermon attacking them. It is the underlying aggressiveness, the attitudes of contempt and force against other people, the experience of suffering from violence stemming from childhood that we must try to eliminate. We must look carefully, thoroughly, and rationally at the experiences of childhood, and we must come out forcefully against those experiences that set the stage for later bigotry and brutality and violence—the symptoms of essential contempt for other people. Spanking a child, with all this implies of our senseless lack of acknowledgment of the child as an important and worthy person, is one of the major predisposing factors in later violence. I believe that unless any present or future National Commission on the Causes and Prevention of Violence looks deeply into the childhood antecedents of this sickness in our society and unless the Commission is brave enough to attack this traditionally American way of raising children, its final report will be worthless. Although much discussion came from the violence of 1968, we still have to *do* something about the problem, not simply outline and describe it.

Speaking in such terms often backfires to the detriment of the speaker. One is accused of all degrees of weakness, abhorrent to our authoritarian, strength-worshiping society, from being soft on communism through representing some particularly disgusting form of passivity, to being, worst of all, an out-and-out dupe or sucker when one attempts to preach a gospel of peace. Two personal experiences come to mind.

Several summers ago I was asked to be a group discussion leader at a two-day church encampment. The theme of the sessions was something like "parent-child relationships," and I was asked to lead the group because I was a child psychologist. The day before we were to leave for the camp, the rector of the church called on me to discuss details of the program, and in the course of his visit learned that neither my wife nor I had ever spanked any of our three children. He saw three affectionate, sunny, well-behaved and very nice children around him all that afternoon and evening, and I was surprised to see that he was surprised. Our mythology, which this gentle and pleasant man shares, has it that children unspanked are impossible and spoiled, and the clear evidence that the myth is not necessarily verified apparently created the kind of conflict within this good man that psychologists call "cognitive dissonance," where one's opinions and the evidence of one's senses come into acute conflict with each other.

The rector is an honest man, and he chose an authentic, though for me unfortunate, means of resolving his cognitive dissonance: he shared his perplexity with the group—all of whom were strangers to me—while introducing me to them the next evening at the camp. His introductory remarks left little question as to his dubiety regarding my earlier off-the-cuff statement about not spanking my children, and they got me off to so bad a start with the group that I had, at the end, to consider the two days much more of a failure than not. The group became instantly hostile, which for most of them lasted throughout the sessions; and I fear that the mythical image of a child psychologist as some kooky, unrealistic, and impractical money scrounger was given additional reinforcement from that moment on for many of them. I myself was saddened that the statement of what I consider a truly Christian principle to an educated and liberal group of Christians—for I do not think of the Protestant Episcopal church as narrow, negative, or fundamentalist in its dogma—should provoke such relatively complete rejection of the principle. It might be said that the group's rejection of me and my principles was based upon their own guilt feelings at having violated Christian principles of "suffering little children" (I wish the verb were less ambiguous), which they could not accept and therefore projected onto me. But it would not be altogether accurate to put it quite this way. I believe that for many of these people spanking children is a legitimate, even God-given means of discipline, which is genuinely effective and sanctioned by all "right-thinking" persons, and that guilt feelings have little or nothing to do with their attitudes.

The second experience occurred at a PTA meeting, after I had spoken, complete with impressive—at least to me—evidence from many experimental studies on child-rearing techniques, about the general uselessness and ineffectiveness of punitive measures. I sensed all too acutely the accumulating atmosphere of outright anger my remarks generated, and was bothered by it. So during the questioning period when I was asked in bitingly hostile tones, "All right, *Doctor*, what would *you* do then if your child deliberately kept on torturing the baby after you'd told him a thousand times to stop it?" I decided on shock treatment. "Spank the little bastard," I said. Instantly all was forgiven. The hall rang with laughter and applause. I was a good guy. I waited out the acclaim, unsmiling, and then said, "And that is exactly what I've been talking about this evening. Your reaction to a statement of unthinking and irresponsible brutality is instant approval. Can't you see that *here*, in you and in your reactions, lies the cause of violence and irresponsibility in your children?"

Now I am not especially proud of my performance or my arrogance that evening, and I still shudder at the memory of the dead and ominous silence that greeted my last words—although it did result in my receiving not a single request to address a PTA group from that time to the present. Come to think of it, I haven't been asked to participate in any subsequent church discussion groups, either. But I did arrive at a point of commitment: to the principle that spanking children is wrong and that it sows the seeds of future violence that we were all, each from his own point of view, deploring with such passion on June 6, 1968.

Beating up children is wrong for many reasons. It creates guilt. Jean Piaget has said, "The sense of guilt is proportional not to the incidental negligence . . . but to physical acts themselves." Spanking lays the groundwork for more and more misconduct, quickly establishing the most vicious of all circles. Kounin and Gump, research psychologists, have recently found that children who had punitive teachers manifested more aggression in their misconduct, were more unsettled and conflicted about misconduct in school, and were less concerned with learning and school-unique values. The authors conclude, "These are not unimportant effects."

Dr. Goodwin Watson states in *What Do We Know About Learning* in 1963:

> Threat and punishment have variable and uncertain effects upon learning. They may make the punished response more likely or less likely to recur; they may set up avoidance tendencies which prevent further learning. . . . Punishment is not, psychologically, the reverse of reward. It disturbs the relationship of the learner to the situation and the teacher. It does not assist the learner in finding and fixing the correct response. . . .
>
> Overstrict discipline is associated with more conformity, anxiety, shyness and acquiescence in children; greater permissiveness is associated with more initiative and creativity. . . . In comparisons of children whose parents were most permissive in home discipline with those whose parents were most strict (both groups of parents loving and concerned), the youngsters from permissive homes showed more enterprise, self-confidence, curiosity, and originality. . . .
>
> Many pupils experience so much criticism, failure, and discouragement in school that their self-confidence, level of aspiration, and sense of worth are damaged. . . . The pupil who sees himself at his worst in school is likely to place little value on study and to seek his role of importance outside the classroom. He may carry through life a sense

of being not good for much. He is likely also to feel resentment at schools, teachers, and books. . . .

When children or adults experience too much frustration, their behavior ceases to be integrated, purposeful, and rational. The threshold of what is "too much" varies; it is lowered by previous failures. . . . Pupils who have had little success and almost continuous failure at school tasks are in no condition to think, to learn, or even to pay attention. *They may turn their anger outward against respectable society* or inward against themselves. (Italics are mine.)

The sources from which I could draw—psychological experiments that are well designed, well controlled, well followed up for validity studies—are endless, and documentation of the simple points that punishment is useless and often dangerous and that it can distort the human being into something capable of assassination is impressively plentiful in psychological literature.

To substitute empirical evidence and scientific knowledge for the prevalent mythology about proper child-rearing techniques would seem to be a part of the answer to the anguished question of today, "What can we do?"

This is a very difficult substitution to make because of our deep-seated reluctances toward looking beneath the superficial aspects of external behaviors, availability of firearms, automation, smog, etc., etc., and especially because of our pathological resistances against accepting personal responsibility for our own behavior.

But let's try. Let's see if the well-publicized outcome of a major research project, one which has caught the attention of the world (which waits with more intensely motivated anticipation for its results than for reports from the first moon explorers), might not help effect the change in child-rearing practices, the negation of antiquated mythologies, and the assumption of personal responsibility for behavior that are needed if we are to prevent Senator Edward Kennedy's murder someday.

The research will be expensive—about the cost of a day or so's fighting in Vietnam. It will require a fairly large staff, a study lasting from three to five years, and cooperation from ministries and departments of education in as many countries as possible —the more the better. It will ask two simple, important questions: What is a good child? and How did he get this way? The questions are important, and the answers—there will be answers, meaningful, practical ones—will solve many of our perplexities. The questions are important too, because they will motivate people to read carefully the answers and to be affected and changed by them. The readers' involvement will be deep, possibly total, because of the questions' intense pertinence to their own lives, their

own children, their friends' lives and children, and
their children's lives and children. The reports from
the first lunar expedition ought to be coming in at
about the same time, and they will be read with nowhere the degree of absorbed fascination—they will
have in no way the same impact upon people's lives
and behavior—that the "Good Child" project will
elicit.

The notion of the research project itself is not complicated, although the demands of the design, also
simple, will be relatively difficult to fulfill. It will not
be impossible. The first step is to find a very large—
in fact, worldwide—sample of young people, pref-
erably sixteen- to eighteen-year-olds, because they
are most apt to be still living at home, which is the
focus of our investigation, and old enough to have
begun establishing those traits of identity which we
shall define as "good." (A less moralistic term could
be found, but the communicative value of "good,"
especially when it will be as carefully defined as is
intended, outweighs its disadvantages.) Let the emphasis upon "good" be noted at once: this is not a
study of abnormality, of deviance. It is a study of
normal, happy, creative, productive, promising young
people. Nor is it a study of minute processes—
reaction times, IQs, test responses and scores,
learning techniques. It is a study of whole young
persons, in all their totality and complexity, insofar
as these can be described and measured by existing

techniques plus those that will have to be devised for the special purposes of the study. We will learn much about these young people, much that we need to know, and it will be a kind of total knowledge. They will live in the pages of the report as they might in a good novel, and their backgrounds, their homes, and their parents will also affect and move the reader with the compelling touch of reality. It will not be difficult to find sizable numbers of the kinds of young people whose happiness, creativity, productivity, achievement, and success in interpersonal relationships are so high as to be the ones we want to focus upon in the study. There are a dozen to a hundred in every high school in our country, and they are indeed an elite group. It is a "blue ribbon" sample we're after, and our researchers, hunting all over the world for these prize boys and girls, will look for a complex of qualities, in which grades and achievement, extracurricular activities—from art to football, student body officer to cheerleader—will be weighted in an inclusive formula which gives appropriate emphasis as well to the number and quality of friendships. It's easier by far to measure grades than quality of friendships, but we will work out a way to make meaningful assessments of the intangibles. They are much more important in defining goodness and authenticity. We will weight community activities, personality attributes and characteristics. And hardest of all, but by that very token, most important, we will finally come up with an index of identity. The assumption here is that the sixteen- to eighteen-year-old boy or girl who has the most firmly established sense of personal identity—who knows best who he is at that point in his life and who can say, "Pretty much regardless of what I'm doing, *I* am the one doing it"—is, other things being equal, the most authentic person we can find and therefore the one most worthy of profound study. This boy or this girl, who emerges with a high score on our formula of achievement, personality traits, creativity, and identity, is the kind of person we would like to have been at that age and that we would like our children to become. He is a worthy model. We will describe him thoroughly, and we will come to know him well.

Our researchers will hunt for these young people. We will consider the recommendations of principals and deans of men and women and coaches of sports and drama, and we will consider very strongly the votes of peers, the student body itself. We will have students in our sample from every part of the country —and, we hope, every part of the world—from every social class and ethnic group, every political, religious, philosophical persuasion, and we will include, to be fair, kids with no persuasions of any kind. We will study the superior dropouts, too, though it will be less convenient to try to get hold of them, for we want our sample to be representative of all authentic late adolescents, and not just those in high school. We will study an equal number of boys and girls, and we would like to study three thousand of them in this country alone, double that amount if our operations can extend abroad.

There would be no trouble in finding this number of young people in the top one to five percent of our "authenticity scale"—the formula weighting the various attributes of goodness we consider important— were it not for one essential criterion these youngsters will have to meet, in addition to the rigorous standards of creativity, warmth, achievement, and identity-formation we're holding them to: each must have a sibling of the same sex, ten to twelve years younger, living at home with the same set of parents who raised the subject. Thus, a superior sixteen-year-old boy, no matter how impressive his qualifications, could not be a part of the experimental group unless he had a four- to six-year-old little brother living at his home with the same mother and father who raised him (we could, and should, use him collaterally, of course, even if he had no such sibling, simply as a rich source of knowledge about superior sixteen-year-olds).

The reason for this criterion lies in Nancy Bayley's finding, in her monumental Berkeley Growth Studies, that certain maternal traits remain remarkably consistent through the years. That is, if a young woman shows such positive or negative traits in dealing with her children as self-confidence, trust and respect for the child, irritability, overprotectiveness, use of threats or bribery or physical punishment to influence the child, and many others, both healthy and unhealthy (it is a sad commentary on the American mothers Bayley studied that the negative traits outweighed by far the positive ones), then she will very likely show these same traits as a middle-aged woman.

We cannot, it seems to me, rely simply on the youngster's or his parents' reports about his background and early experiences if we are to answer clearly and scientifically the second question, "How did he get this way?" Although it would surprise me if the parents of such authentic youngsters would deliberately falsify reports on how they raised the children, since I doubt that children of liars can easily become authentic, at least at so young an age as sixteen, we cannot ignore the distorting effects of time itself, the ease with which often very important events and experiences are forgotten. No, we must have an on-the-spot coverage, and Bayley's data may make it possible to assume that, by and large, the way our sixteen-year-old's mother treats her six-year-old son is similar enough to the way she treated the older boy as he was growing up to give us a direct look, coevally, at the older boy's past and present. This technique will allow us the most reliable answer we can get to the question of how superior functioning is encouraged in the home.

Such a technique involves living-in observers, and again we are in luck: some recent studies indicate that after a while the presence of an outsider in the home, especially if he is accepting, relatively unobtrusive, and definitely not intrusive, does not seem to affect significantly the major variables being studied. This is fortunate, and we shall, initially, rely upon this factor. If it proves not to be workable, then again we must come up with something else, so as to get as uncontaminated a picture of life in a given home as possible. Assuming the family's cooperation —and I do: indeed, I should think the presence in the home of the "Good Child" researchers would be a most prestigious feather in the family's cap—it will not be hard to solve the problem.

There is only one way to answer the anguished question, Why? Why violence, why assassinations, why the repetitive, cyclical slaughters of young men? The answer does not lie, all too obviously, in peace conferences, armament or disarmament programs, "law and order" as a repressive measure, or in the *ad hoc, post hoc,* punitive, idealistic, or any other sorts of ideas and techniques tried for centuries with so dismal a record of success. The answer lies in research—large-scale, long-term, expensive (but so economical!), controlled research focused upon the inner and outer factors that make children—and later, adults—hate. Wars and assassinations and cruel punishment have economic and cultural and ideological causes as well, of course, and it would be oversimplifying to assert that identifying the psychological causes will eliminate such stigmas on our civilization. But the psychological factors—the fears, the frustrations, the resentments and jealousies and envies, the rages and the hatreds and the hostilities— are the catalysts that spark situations, which otherwise could easily be solved or transcended by intelligent men of good will, into uncontrolled disaster.

The "Good Child" research program may not be successful as an approach to answering our questions; there are many ways to try, and there are many inventive men and women who, given time and opportunities, can find still better ways. But we must try something—for anxious, waiting passivity has never been a solution to any problem, whether personal or international. Whatever the approach, it is bound to identify the qualities not just of hurting, hating children that predispose them to later violence but also the qualities that helped to create these distinguished, thoughtful, happy youngsters who are the promise of a civilized future. At the moment, many of our finest young people are dropping out of a society that, instead of acknowledging and respecting their high ethical and value systems, berates, derides, and persecutes them. The countries that accept those of this group who expatriate themselves are the richer for their new citizens. We are the losers. A nation that boasts these young people and finds means of understanding and supporting them, such that they will be honored and that *their* children will be like them, will come to deserve them.

XI:
The Institutions

No child has ever been helped by any organized religious body carrying out its official functions. Children have been bored and confused by their churches. They have been frightened, made to feel guilty, and have been given misinformation and distorted ideas. They have been lied to, and they have been patronized. Not too long ago they were castrated, tortured, sacrificed. They have been herded into bloody and tragic wars, to be slaughtered, uncomprehending and weeping, all in the name of their churches. They have been unjustly charged with the vilest accusations of sin and crime. The most perverted and inhuman forms of discipline and penance have been forced upon them. The churches enclose children in narrow prisons of proscriptions and negative commandments, instead of opening up their lives to free communion. All that is healthy and admirable in children—their spontaneity, their honesty, their dignity—has been subjected to systematic attempts by the churches to destroy it. Fortunately, a fourth strength of childhood, resilience, has prevented the churches' total success.

The innumerable instances when children *have* been helped in church—comforted, cared for, educated, helped toward a feeling of strength, led to understanding of, compassion for, and communion with others—have all been the results not of church doctrine, but of decent, compassionate, and wise persons in the church, who are expressing their own decency, compassion, and wisdom in relation to the children. There are many such persons connected with every other institution, from the schools to the courts, to which children are exposed, and it is to their and the church people's credit as human beings, not as representatives of their institutions, that the children are helped.

The reason that the official church cannot really help children, no matter how benign its outlook, how intensive its youth program, is that the church, by its very nature, is committed to an abstraction, and children do not think abstractly. The monumental work of Jean Piaget, a Swiss developmental psychologist, throughout the last forty years has shown us convincingly what we have always known: that a child for the first seven to twelve years of his life (and to the end of his life, if he has only average intelligence) thinks in concrete terms. He thinks of things, and he can think of combinations of things, such that he is capable of much mathematical thought. But his attempts at thinking *beyond* things, at thinking of their causal, as opposed just to their, say, additive, relationships, are so shot through with illogicalities, inconsistencies, intrusive fantasies, and grossly inaccurate perceptions as to fall far short of the abstraction required for thinking clearly about concepts such as "God." We smile at hearing a child recite, "Hail, Mary, full of grapes," but it is a vivid example of a child's concretism. A glowing Madonna full of grapes may be a bit unusual, but then, most things adults say don't bear up under much examination either, and it's usually best just to accept them or not to think about them. The parroting of pledges and prayers, lofty and character-building as we may think them to be ("not thinking about" our own utter impenetrability to their themes when we were young), is a shameful reduction of beautiful imagery and profound thought to the level of a television commercial. The concept of "grace," like the concept of God, is majestic. One would think the churches would have more self-respect than to allow their majestic themes, which only an adult mind can begin to grasp, to be cheapened into sugar-coated, meaningless little recitations and fairy tales. If the church is content to teach children morality without frightening them, and a sense of beauty, which the liturgies of the older religions, at least, possess to a degree that will serve as a serene and evocative respite from the stridency of everyday affairs throughout the child's life, then it does its job fairly well. But if the church's goal is also to instill in children wonder, and awe, and the self-transcending sense of unity with something more powerful than oneself, then it fails miserably. It cannot succeed at this, because of the very nature of a child's ideation; and the crucial failing of the church has lain not only in its inability to recognize the impossibility of communicating abstract concepts but in its attempts to force this communication with unreal fairy tales and meaningless recitations. It is also why so many young people leave the church and, for a time at least, abandon their "faith"—which was never real faith but just an accommodation to what their elders said.

The truly religious person—as opposed to those who are fanatically religious or neurotically religious, who are as concrete-minded in their religions as a child, never having progressed beyond the gory preoccupations of childhood and the exclusive emphases upon behavior (usually forbidden behavior, which is enticing to them) to the adult and abstract, yet real, attitudes of compassion for all humankind and a search for inner tranquility—is saddened by the self-destructive behavior of organized religion. He regrets seeing so many young people driven from the church, by its outmoded obtuseness, with the greater than fifty percent probability of their never returning, for he knows how helpful, how soaringly growth-induc-

ing, to the individual and to society, a temple for
adults can be.

A class of twenty-five college freshmen, seventeen
and eighteen years old, is discussing religion. They
have come to know each other fairly well, and they
like their professor. They are intense, likable, intelligent young people, and they speak for their generation, articulately and thoughtfully. They speak for
each other, too, for they are very young, and they
want to impress, or at least to be noticed, if not liked
and respected. They are not as sure of themselves as
they may sound; but they are becoming more so, as
they find that they can say things previously unspeakable and that the things they say are listened to, and
evaluated, and criticized, and accepted, and supported. They are coming to know themselves, and
their tentative opinions are becoming incorporated
into their personality structures. They are becoming
real.

Carla, a pretty farm girl, starts off. "I know it's awful to say, but I don't believe in going to church. I
guess I believe in God, but I'm not even sure of that.
But I am sure I won't ever go to church again. I can't
stand it, to see people come out hating, just as much
as they did when they went in."

Barbara speaks up. "I know what you mean. I went
to church with my folks yesterday, and as we walked

out, my mother said how sick it made her to see Mrs. So-and-so playing up to the minister."

Eddie, an intense young man, product of a Catholic preparatory education, breaks in. "Oh, come on, those are just *people*. What do they have to do with religion?"

The class explodes, and it takes ten minutes for individual voices to be heard. Finally Luke, another Catholic boy, comes over. "Damn it, Eddie's right! The church *doesn't* care about people! All it wants is to turn us into good Catholics, not good people!"

"Well, the Methodists are worse," Faye says. "They don't even care if we're good Methodists. They just want us to be good *machines!*"

Frank, a Negro, looks at her. "You should be a Southern Baptist, baby."

Everyone laughs, and the tension is dissipated for a moment. Stephen, a handsome, bearded boy, speaks. "Well, I'm a Jew. And I think I *have* been taught that it's all right to be a person. So why is it that it's really hard for me to tell you that I'm Jewish?"

The class is silent. They look at the professor. He controls an impulse to lecture on anti-Semitism and instead asks quietly, "Well? Why *was* it hard for Stephen?"

Silence. The professor looks at his favorite student, a bright and usually articulate girl. "Jenny?"

"Gee, I don't . . . Well, of course I know. Jews know

that they're looked down on in our society. Or they think they are. Actually, Stephen makes me mad. I think he's asking for sympathy or something. That's dumb. He's the smartest kid in the class, and he knows it, and he knows we all know it. I don't think it's fair to blame his religion for his own problems."

Sylvia, an extremely pretty girl, has, as usual, been paying very little attention to the discussion. But at Jenny's remarks she stiffened into rapt concentration. In the silence that follows, Sylvia utters a heart-felt "Whew!" that focuses the class's delighted attention upon her; it is the first time Sylvia has joined any discussion. She flushes and gestures self-consciously, as if to brush them all away. Still they focus on her.

"Oh, for heaven's sakes!" she mumbles, feeling trapped into expression and at the same time relieved and pleased at the commitment her exclamation has made. Now she has to speak, as her classmates' eyes still hold her own; she senses a mounting excitement at the realization that for the first time in her life she is about to take a stand. "Well, what I meant . . . was . . . was that I think Jenny was right. I think people *do* blame their religions for their own problems. Like my . . . like a lady I know. She thinks that . . . that all kinds of things are really bad. Because her religion says they are. But really, she just doesn't like them herself, so it's real convenient to quote scripture against them. That way, she doesn't have to *do* them . . . You know. And all the time, she thinks she's real . . . saintly, or something. You know?"

Eric, smooth and cool, smiles. "You're talking about your mother, and you're talking about sex. Yeah, we know. But the point is, religion is *supporting* your mother in her hangups. Now, what kind of a religion is that?"

Jeff is a boy fiercely involved in everything that comes up. He shouts, "That's *every* kind of religion! That's what they're *all* for, to support people's flip-outs! It makes them feel superior to everyone else, and it makes them not afraid to die. Except it doesn't work, because my great-grandmother is the holiest old roller you've ever seen, and she's scared . . . to *death* of dying. Well, I don't think we *need* to be scared of dying. Unless we haven't lived, like my great-grandmother. She's had a bad, bad life, and I don't blame her for being afraid to die. As far as she knows, no matter what her Bible tells her, it's just going to be more of the same old misery."

Frank speaks up again. "My people have had bad lives, too. All they had was their religion, to give them comfort. I don't know what they would have done without it, without really believing that in Heaven they'd be free of all the crap they had to take down here."

Sylvia, now an eager participant in the group, rushes to speak. "But, Frank, that's just my point!

Maybe if the Blacks *hadn't* had their religion, they would have started improving their lives down here a long time ago, like they're finally doing now."

Frank begins, "That's easy to say, but—" when Jeff interrupts. "She's right, and you know it. That's what really bugs me about religion. All these old guys saying, Do this and especially Don't do that, and Be nice, and Don't make waves, and Remember how sinful and stupid you are. God! It's worse than the Nazis! Damn it, I want to learn to be *proud* of myself, not wallow in that stinking humility all my life!"

Eric looks at Sylvia, then coldly at Jeff. "I don't think there's much danger of that. You've got your share of pride. But what happens when you wake up to the fact that you *don't* know everything? Will you be too stiff-necked with pride to admit that God knows more than you?"

Jeff glares. "I'll *learn* what I don't know. I won't turn into a pious hypocrite like you. You're . . . you're *arrogant* with all those smooth little clichés about that old myth called God."

Robin reacts to Eric's flushed face and clenched fists. She considers herself a conciliator, and she is deathly afraid of direct encounters. "Now come on, Jeff," she hurries to say. "That isn't very nice. Just because Eric doesn't agree with you is no reason to call him arrogant and hypocritical."

Jenny is furious at Robin's mediation in what promised to be a good fight and turns on her. "Look,

Miss Pollyanna, what's so terrible about expressing an opinion? Why don't *you* try it for once instead of being so wishy-washy? Come on, what *do* you think? Do you believe in God?"

Robin's eyes overflow at the attack. She cannot speak for a moment and looks desperately at the professor for help. He smiles but remains silent, and she finds choked words. "I . . . I don't think I have to answer that. A person's beliefs are . . . are private."

Jenny is adamant. "What about everyone else? *They're* saying what they believe in. Don't you respect them for that?"

Robin looks down. She sighs, long and deep, and silence in the classroom is absolute. When she does speak, it sounds as if she has aged ten years. "No," she whispers. "No, I don't." Her voice strengthens, and she looks around at her classmates, looks directly at them. "I *don't* believe in God." She can't suppress a timorous glance upward, as if expecting a thunderbolt from Heaven. The class giggles, understanding all too well her involuntary posture. Robin giggles, too, and in a moment they are all rolling in hilarity. Even Eric succumbs, and wiping tears of laughter away, calls out, "Good for you, Robin!"

We may leave the freshmen at this point, full of their ringing sincerity, aware that their youthful ideas are still unmodified by experience, perhaps regretting that religion seems little more than a joke to them, but mostly convinced that for most of them religion has become a mixture of hypocrisy and farce with nothing meaningful to say. We cannot easily condemn these bright young people, and we know we could not, even if we wanted to, convert or revert them to the tenuous beliefs of their younger years. We are forced to the conclusion, perhaps reluctantly, but so convincingly that no other conclusion is possible, that their churches have failed them. They have moved beyond authoritarianism; they are on the road toward humanism, toward the stimulation in interpersonal encounter that they have never found sitting passively throughout a sermon. And it is quite possible that deeply within ourselves we envy these young people for what they are experiencing and what they have found. We may well wish, in spite of ourselves, that we had had this kind of interpersonal stimulation when we were seventeen and eighteen. Perhaps we would be freer, less hating, today. Perhaps our understanding of each other would be deeper, not so circumscribed by judgment and moralism as to keep us from all but the most superficial contact with each other—and with our youngsters.

The churches have killed God for these young people. They may have deprived them of something infinitely important.

. . .

The schools do a little better in their stated purpose, the education of children, than the churches do
in theirs, but the fact that school attendance is required by law—a rigid condition that completely
overlooks a child's natural eagerness to learn and to
be associated with interested adults—is both the
school's unfair advantage and its shame. Less than
half of all students, financially and intellectually
qualified, go from high school to college, and this
shocking statistic can be blamed directly upon the
schools. To turn a questing, eager, pliable intelligence
into one so overgrown with dislike, boredom, outright
hatred of the whole learning process, and self-defeat-
ism that it could not even consider applying for college admission is no small achievement. The schools
have all too clearly demonstrated their hellish ability
to do just this, with too many youngsters. A young
man, a high school dropout, reports, "The sisters put
hair ribbons in my hair whenever I was bad and made
me parade around at recess. Now I understand what
they must have thought about femininity, to degrade
it so, but then, God, how I hated them!"

Another boy, failing in school, says, "Yeah, I used
to like school. About the third grade. But I wouldn't
understand something, and I'd ask, and the teachers
would always say, 'You've got good intelligence, so
you should understand. You just don't want to.' And
then they'd punish me."

Another dropout, named Carter: "My history teacher got laughs by calling me 'Farter' in class. He had a great time. I used to die."

Another comment, from a particularly perceptive dropout: "My teachers would always send me and the other kids to the principal's office when we were bad. And I figured—what weak slobs they were, not to be able to handle anything themselves. The dopes, they couldn't even see that we were *asking* them to be strong. They flunked the test every time. This was what a college education does to you? Not for me!"

A comment heard hundreds of times: "My junior high teachers all the time kept yelling about how hard college was, so we had to work real hard then to get ready. But we knew they were just telling us how great *they* were, to have got through it. I think that's disgusting."

The fortunate child (the one who goes on to college, where his chance of meeting more admirable representatives of education is slightly higher) is he whose parents, in their authenticity, their lack of the phoniness so tellingly demonstrated in the comments above, compensate for the inadequacies and the inadequates he finds in his elementary and secondary years. They show him another way, that learning is not necessarily a painful, humiliating, degrading experience but rather an exciting and immediately rewarding one. Such parents are, sadly, in the minority, for it seems mostly to be the accepted response to side automatically with the teacher in his thoughtless punitiveness, which shows no effect of whatever "New Methods in Education" courses he may have taken, and to assume the child is wrong. This, of course, simply reinforces the child's contempt for education.

The story is the same in reverse: the hostile parent, unable to accept his own or his child's real deficiencies, who blames the teacher and the school system *in toto*, similarly reinforces his child's contempt for education.

Teachers reenact their own educational experiences, in spite of their college education, just as parents reenact their own parents' child-rearing techniques, in spite of personal psychotherapy that has finally enabled them to break free from their parents' influence. The teacher who can transcend his past, who can wholeheartedly bring his own insight and his own knowledge of newer and better, and more honest, ways of dealing with children, is a magnificent example for them. We can, usually, count on the fingers of one hand teachers of this superior kind that we have had.

Juvenile courts also, all too often, present a model of inauthenticity to young people, and it seems particularly indefensible here because the young people they influence are themselves, almost by definition, already inauthentic. At worst, juvenile courts commit two common and serious errors: they moralize and lecture, on the basis of the judge's own biases, which incredibly often are so bigoted as to be laughable, if it were a laughing matter; or they excuse and deny the youngster's responsibility in the offense at hand.

To say bitingly that long hair is the cause of juvenile delinquency is to betray an ignorance of psychological and sociological principles of causation so profound as to be ludicrous. Yet one sees it in print every day. To attenuate punishment for a vicious and deliberate crime on the basis of the perpetrator's youth is similarly to prove oneself ignorant of cause and effect, action-and-consequence relationships. Neither, obviously, works, although both are used daily in courts across the nation, as witnessed by the sixty percent recidivism rate of young offenders.

Lacking a juvenile court presided over by a judge versed in the psychological and sociological influences upon his charges—or, at least, one who tries to learn them before passing judgment—one can only conclude that the courts are increasing crime, even as the churches are increasing the incidence of atheism and the schools are increasing detestation of education. In all cases, the institution itself is inauthentic. It clings to worn-out, unscientific tenets based more upon emotionalism and bias than upon thoughtful observation and experimentation. Its representatives are inauthentic people, who impose their biases, and sometimes their emotional problems, upon the children who should be the objects of their professional concern.

There are, of course, many proud exceptions—churches, schools, and courts whose dispositions of their charges are kind and honest and realistic. To say in 1969 that these exceptions are in the minority is a shocking charge. But it is true. Most children cannot become authentic in an inauthentic society, and to the extent that society's institutions rely upon myth, fear, and personal distortion to pass on their values to the young, to that extent is the society inauthentic.

Our children deserve more; they deserve at least the opportunity of an undistorted climate in which to develop. Honesty cannot grow in the midst of deceit, and courage does not spring from fear. Our churches can concentrate upon morality and aesthetics, our schools can stress the thrill of learning, our courts can emphasize responsibility and honesty. They cannot do these things without people who themselves embody these goals. There are many such people, and our children deserve association with them. The handful of stimulating teachers we recall, the perceptive probation officer who sees the young offender as both bewildered and culpable and who makes his recommendations accordingly, the priest whose life epitomizes his preaching—they are the most valuable resources in our society, and it is they, and their peers in every other vocation, in their pitiful rarity, who have elevated our society occasionally to the heights of maturity it should consistently reach. President John F. Kennedy was such an authentic model: he lived honesty and responsibility and courage, and we were all better for his life. The shame and horror of his death give awful awareness both of contingency in all our lives and of the rarity of so integrated a man.

XII:
The Levels of Loving

A recent *New Yorker* cartoon shows a middle-aged woman standing with her husband outside a Broadway theater and saying to a friend, "I'm beginning to think everybody in the whole world is preoccupied with sex except Henry and me."

As a gently satiric observer of the contemporary scene, *The New Yorker* is peerless. There are truths hitting us in this cartoon, barbed yet jocund, and they seem to cover the range of sexuality in our time—Henry's wistful acceptance of the absence of sex in his life, his wife's unknowing denial of it, her confidence that others will support her, and all the while, in the garish background, are the ever-present, graphic voices of sexuality feared, sexuality longed for, sexuality forbidden, sexuality enthroned. Only rarely do we see sexuality enjoyed, and the dry data of divorce corroborate our impression of the rarity of sexual happiness. "Cold and indifferent," "mental cruelty," "incompatibility," "adultery," "inability to

live as husband (wife)," "abandonment"—this is the
script of the tragedy of the marital bedroom, and it
describes in varying degrees of candor marriage's
antagonists: impotence and frigidity.

We teach our children almost deliberately to become impotent husbands and frigid wives, and we
condemn them, by our teaching, to empty lives, to
divorce, to fantasies of longed-for sex that effectively
replace the warm reality of fulfilled sex. We set up
our grandchildren for the same aridity, too, in our
teachings. And all the while, the strident clamor of
publicized, artificial sex sounds louder in our ears,
seems sweeter in our fantasies—and those of our
children and our grandchildren—and its din splits
us farther from our sexual self to a bewildering self
of ineffectiveness, perversion, coldness. The hidden
agenda of sexual hangup is responsible not only for
the majority of divorces, but also for most suicides,
most mental illnesses, most cases of obesity and skin
disorder, and maybe even lung cancer. Unresolved
sexual tensions lead to smoking, too. It's a safe bet
that the ashtrays in psychiatrists' offices are more
frequently emptied than those in, say, obstetricians'
offices. (This does not, to be sure, explain the especially good taste of a cigarette after successful sexual
union—or after a good dinner, for that matter. Perhaps the popularity of cigarette smoking, obdurate
in the face of all common sense, lies in its ability to
satisfy needs at many levels.)

Let us examine the curriculum that leads to degrees in impotence, frigidity, perversion:

A mother who is an R.N. and is noted in the community for her cleanliness comments offhandedly one night to her fourteen-year-old son that his girl friend had come that afternoon into the doctor's office where the mother works. "My goodness, you should have seen her underwear!" she says. "It was filthy! Why, I was shocked!"

The boy cannot know his mother's jealousy of the pretty girl, her withering knowledge of the beginning of his transfer of affection away from her. But he cannot help, with his "training" in cleanliness, but look at the girl in school the next day with a guilty revulsion. The girl will never understand his sudden coolness, and her own self-image may well suffer a confused wrench.

A young father says, half-defensively, half-proudly, "No, I don't cuddle my sons. I never did. It's O.K. for girls, but . . . well, you know. Besides, I figure they'd lose respect for me and wouldn't obey me." The father might have added, "And my father never did that sort of stuff with me."

His wife, listening, thinks of his staccato, loveless lovemaking and wonders if it is, after all, so wrong to infuse little boys with warmth and tenderness. It might be this same father who, several years later, after the divorce, is chiefly responsible for the change in his now ten-year-old son from clinging effeminacy to normal boyishness. A divorced father who honors his visitation rights and, even if rarely, devotes a day or a weekend solely to his child, is far better than a resident father who ignores and/or browbeats the child consistently.

To give time ungrudgingly to someone is to love him, for time is the most precious commodity we have, and the gift of time is far more solid, more durable, more meaningful than any toy or bequest. When time that could be spent with children is spent on golf courses, at bridge tables, in bars, in front of television sets, then it is clear where love lies: with the self. The self may well need this love, this indulgence, and it may even be strengthened thereby to offer more love to the children later—or so the rationalization goes. It is a rationalization, because the hoarding of love, as self-indulgence, increases its inaccessibility, and that of the golfer, the bridge player, the TV addict. (When these parents get home, they have to catch up on office work, or clean the house—and years go by with no real contact between them and the children, until finally the children are grown and gone.) It is a rationalization because the capacity for intimacy, an ingredient of mature love for which there is no substitute, is lived only in intimacy. The child who has an intimate relationship with his parents grows to become an adult intimate with his spouse. The forgotten child, seeking satisfaction of his need for intimacy in nonhuman activities or inappropriate humans—the movie-goer or TV addict, the bookworm, the daydreamer; or the bully, the hanger-on, the delinquent gang member, the buyer of affection and belongingness—this child grows into the self-indulgent adult, unable to come close to his children, unable to love. Often he seeks in a psychotherapist the human relationship he missed as a child and seems unable to establish as an adult. For the fifty minutes he is there, his need is fulfilled. But the "hour" ends, and there is another, hated, patient waiting.

Still basically unfulfilled, apparently never to be satisfied, the need for intimacy must be deadened, for it is too painful, it has lasted too long. The addictions deaden—alcohol, tranquilizers, food, television, golf, bridge, doctors' appointments—but they do not really erase, so they must be continued. Justifying their use as being necessary to clear the mind, to rest, to prepare for real intimacy with the kids later is sheer rationalization, for the end is just the opposite: further alienation from the very intimacy that would solve the lifelong problem.

If an alienated person, one without ties of intimacy to another, is fortunate enough to have children, the solution to his problem lies in them, not in a thera-

pist's office (except to start him off on the road toward
intimacy), and certainly not in the wealth of addic-
tive products our society offers so abundantly. It is
not exploiting a child to use him to solve our problem, if in doing so he derives the same reward that we
do. On the contrary, it is the mutual experience of
intimacy of child and adult, in the attempts of each
to satisfy his own and the other's need, that, in diminishing alienation, fulfills them both.

The specifics of the mutuality of intimacy between
adult and child depend, of course, upon the personalities and the opportunities involved. It is not the intent
here to offer a "how to" guide. Indeed, the very spirit
of the existential approach, which holds that the
spontaneous flowering of intimacy between persons
is the only real and meaningful basis for love, would
be grossly violated by the structured and inauthentic
artificiality of such a guide. Guides do not work, and
they often backfire most destructively, simply because they are guides, and thereby insult the fresh
immediacy of human experience. It essentially mat-
ters surprisingly little what a parent does in relation
to a child. Some of the happiest children come from
homes whose practices have deliberately or inad-
vertently broken every "rule" of child-raising, and
some of the most miserable children are those raised
by the book. What does matter is the attitude and the
quality with which a child is raised. If the attitude is
compounded of love and respect and joy in the child,

then the techniques are laughably irrelevant. And if the attitude is one of grudging resentment, then all the "good" or approved—or even existential—techniques in the world will be useless.

For intimacy, for love, time is required. What, then, of the pathetic boast of the mother of a fire-setting child, "But he *knows* we love him! He goes everywhere with us, and if he can't, we don't go! Do you know, we've never had a baby sitter? We are both completely devoted to him! He's our whole life!"

To indulge oneself and to deny oneself are two quite different things. The former, self-indulgence, bespeaks the narcissism born of emptiness and isolation, the neurotic attempt to satisfy the needs for attention, affection, and intimacy that were never satisfactorily met by one's parents. Self-indulgence denies others, in its insatiable search for something to fill the void within. Self-denial, as witnessed by the phrase, "We've never had a baby-sitter," is equally neurotic, but the dynamics are different. Here, the person is saying, "I am unimportant, insignificant. My life, my feelings, my opinions don't count. I *can* count only through others."

The person who denies himself must live vicariously if there is to be any meaning at all in his life. He must focus his authentic, but too feared, need for meaning upon someone else, and in the focusing, may overburden, even smother, him. The deepest need, the most potent, the very basis of every man's psychology, is the need for meaning. "I count, I am important, *I am of value!*" Every retarded child, every case of senile dementia in every back ward of every mental hospital, every Skid Row resident, every movie star, every man, woman, and child is saying, every moment, "My life means something!"

It is to prove this statement, to validate it, that we go on living. We work, and we love, and we speak of ourselves. The validation is sometimes perverse, as in self-assertion through crime, but it can all be seen as testament to personal significance. It is not an easy task to prove one's worth, and it becomes even less easy if, at the same time, we are required to testify to someone else's worth as well. The child who, by his life and achievement, has to embody and prove the wisdom and good practices of his parents is doubly and triply burdened. It is small wonder that such a child often rebels, sets fires, steals. He finds accurately the weak spots in his weak, self-denying parents, and he burrows deeply into them. It is an impressive display of the tactics of revenge.

But more impressive, and even more pathetic than the little boy setting fires, unshouldering thereby his parents' demands that he prove their devotion to the world, is the appallingly acute demonstration of love backfired. Love rooted in narcissism, whether it is the frantic void-filling narcissism of the self-indulgent parent or the vicarious search for meaning through a child of the self-denying parent, is love backfired:

it leads to anguish and recrimination and a widening of the space between the lover and the loved. Narcissism—self-love that is not love—is the antithesis of the calm ability to give unqualified, unconditional, unrecriminating love that stems from self-respect. Narcissism is self-disrespect, and it comes masked as arrogance and vanity and painful susceptibility to real and imagined affronts to all too easily wounded pride. The father insisting upon "respect" from his children, the mother demanding instant obedience from a child who genuinely wants to please but is, because he is a questing human being also, temporarily distracted or concentrating with everything he has upon something else—these parents are terribly vulnerable. Their narcissism is going to be threatened by what they interpret as disrespect and disobedience, and they are going to strike out, immediately, destructively, verbally and physically, at the villainous children.

The children are not villains. It has never consciously occurred to them to view their parents in any way other than as the bedrock of security they are. This is the view common to all children, though cruelly shattered in some, and it encompasses respect and love and obedience and wish to please. The secure parent knows his importance to his child and therefore does not need to insist that the child prove it every day. The insecure, narcissistic parent, untrustful of himself and therefore unknowing of his vital importance to the child, will require daily or hourly demonstrations, in the form of "respect" or "obedience," and he will never be satisfied. Further, in his neurotic demands, he will ultimately prove to the child that he cannot be counted upon, that he is not a bedrock of security for the child, and that he does not warrant respect or obedience. And then, he will really not get it. Again, we see the insidious transmission of insecurity from generation to generation, for it is the child of this narcissistic parent, who has learned not to trust, who may lose trust in himself as well and become himself a narcissistic parent.

A meaningful relationship between parent and child, one in which each feels free to accept and to express his natural, undistorted trust in the other, is the one that allows the child real love and loving in adulthood. Meaningful love has been characterized earlier as consisting of communication, intimacy, and passion, and it is also composed of liking, abandon, and respect. Meaningful love is a concrete, immediate experience, in spite of the highly abstract words just used to characterize it, such that it is stronger in the presence of the loved one than when he is absent. It is not love that grows by separation: it is "romance" and idealization, often an unreal, even distorted idealization of the absent lover or child. Love that expands and fulfills and gives meaning to the immediate moment, so that the day, in retrospect, is a good one, comes from the direct encounter between people. The out-of-town husband, the golfing mother, the teacher or the student missing a class, the child away at summer camp can all love those from whom they are parted, but such distant love is virtually unreal compared with the present appreciation of a wife's or a child's smile of affection, a classroom's laughter or absorption in the meaningful and, yes, passionate communication between teacher and students.

These are the levels of loving, different in their degrees of intimacy, but alike in their communion and mutuality of appreciation. These are the delights of the day, the sustained moments of meaningfulness that accumulate, day after day, into the fully lived life. If we can love at even one level, our life has value, and it is enough that we live, and love. We need not ask for goals or purpose. If we can love not at all —if there is no one whom we trust completely, no one with whom we can be completely open, no one who, by his presence, provokes our spontaneous delight; no one in whose presence we can abandon all our controls, all our defenses, in an unguarded passion of intimacy—then there is no value, no meaning to our life. The businessman suspicious of his colleagues and his employees, the husband suspicious of his wife, the teacher threatened by her pupils, the parent resentful and punitive toward his children—these do not love, and it is not surprising that they leave their jobs dissatisfied, go home from work depressed and to bed exhausted, welcome the leavetakings of their family, seek respite from life in sleep and drugs and meaningless stimulation for its own sake. With love, life is a welcomed thing. With love at many levels— when there is meaningful interchange with children and clients and bosses and students and friends and family throughout the day—only then is life fully lived.

XIII:
The Masks of Despair

Man grows according to his interpretation
of his self.

—Victor Frankl

A young mother, her face frozen unpleasantly into a sullen expression of unhappiness, her make-up serving not to enhance her looks but grotesquely emphasizing the stiff, almost inhuman face behind it, continues her complaints about her child's disobedience.

A young man, his expression unchangingly fierce, his brows contracted into what seems a perpetual frown, bewails his inability to act naturally with his fiancée. "I think she's going to break our engagement. She says I'm so stiff she doesn't think I can ever relax. I do love her, but I get so tied up whenever I'm with her that I *can't* relax!"

A bruised child stares fixedly at his storming father, trying to stay as unblinkingly emotionless as he can, knowing how infuriating (but not knowing how guilt-producing) his tears are to the father.

These are masks of despair we wear, the facial protections against being touched, being reached—they are the facial cages that hold within them, unseen, the thwarted expressions of our feelings. The masks are the symbols of defeat. "I cannot reveal in my face, my exposed, vulnerable face, what I feel, because I'm afraid of what might happen if I do. I'll be laughed at, or scorned. Someone, seeing love on my face, will exploit it, and use me. If he sees fear, or hate, he'll turn it against me, and it'll just be worse for me in the end.

"I don't want to go through life pouting, or frowning, or like a wax figure. I'm *human!* I want to show I'm human! But I can't. I can't take a chance."

The people behind the masks of despair are unfree. They are bound. They are inauthentic. They are confining their humanity to a single facial expression, an expression which denies their humanity and which alienates them more and more, every moment they wear the expression, from their humanity. They are fortified and imprisoned by their "body armor" (as Wilhelm Reich calls it), a vivid metaphor for the stiffness and tension of people in bondage.

The people behind the masks long to be free, to be spontaneous, and it is awesome and gratifying to see the masks split and their humanity emerge when the longing is acknowledged. The young mother's friend says simply, "You really hate yelling at Bobby, don't you? You just want to love him." A look of startled, then relieved, womanliness shines in the mother's eyes. Her pout disappears, and her make-up blends with her face. A human being shows through: a lovely, conflicted young woman, suddenly feeling relief—and hope.

The roommate of the scowling young man says, "You know, I've been reading about some of this sensory awakening stuff from Esalen. It's sort of like Yoga, I think. Try it. They say you've got to localize your tension first. Where is it? Your face, right? O.K., then you've got to realize you're the one who's tensing yourself up. Barbara isn't; *you* are. O.K.? Yeah, I know you know all that. Just go along with it for a second. O.K.? Now: close your eyes and *experience* your face. Let your consciousness move to your face. It sounds weirdo, but it's easy. Do it. Now just sit there a minute, feeling your face from inside . . . Tom! You're smiling!"

The storming father experiences a sudden clutch, a braking of his angry attack upon his expressionless son. (He describes it later to his stunned wife, "I don't know, but all of a sudden I saw myself there, set for a blow, not flinching, but scared to death." Sudden tears blind the father. His arms turn from tools of torture to comforting supports, and he hugs the boy, saying, "I scared you, didn't I, son? I'm sorry. I'm sorry." In their shared tears the son and the father reexperience their humanity, their compassion, their courage. They are free now to make something rewarding out of their relationship.

To be free is to acknowledge one's humanity, one's basic goodness, one's essential strength. To free a child so that he can grow unencumbered toward real maturity is to acknowledge his humanity and to be touched and delighted by it. Humanity is feeling and expressing; it is spontaneity; it is working and thinking and solving problems and making choices. It is loving.

Humanity is attenuated by fears, and it is stifled by tension. The masks of despair suffocate their wearers, leaving them pallid, anoxic, one-track programmed machines. Their behavior is predictable because it is inhuman, but herein lies the appeal of inhumanity. We seem to wish to be able to predict, and hence to control, our children's behavior and their very thoughts, not recognizing that in doing so, we dehumanize them.

J. F. T. Bugental, in his *Challenges of Humanistic Psychology*, defends his human-oriented approach by contrasting it with the machine-like approach of more traditional (behavioristic) psychology: ". . . where behavioristic psychology has taken as its goals the attainment of the ability to describe, to predict, and to control . . . humanistic psychology seeks to so describe men and their experiences that they will be better able to predict and control their *own* experiences (and thus, implicitly, to resist the control of others)."

We can predict and control our own behavior only if we are free to do so, free from the neurotic bondage of denied humanity. A parent, proud, almost unbelieving, says of his child, "Look what he did! He taught me that I can do it, too!"

It doesn't matter what the child did—he showed courage, probably, or he spoke earnestly, or he expressed love. It does matter that his parent saw and recognized the child's humanity and that the impact of the recognition was so great as to reawaken his own.

Developmental freedom, the theme of this book, is the condition of humanity. The child who develops in freedom, who is free to express, free to love, free to choose, and equally free to inhibit his expression, to hate, to be dependent upon the direction of his parents—this child, whether two or twenty, is fully human, and his life has meaning. When he becomes a parent he will grant, gladly, this same freedom to his children, and he will not fear their becoming spoiled or unmanageable or delinquent. He knows the confident strength of his own controls over himself that have been nurtured and rehearsed from within on his life and their independent and reliable functioning right now.

The free parent is not as rare as one might think. In every schoolroom, every campus in the country, are many children and young people who work well and industriously, who love their learning and who express this love in their projects, their independent studies—and in their passionate questioning of, and dialogues with, their teachers. These are the youngsters whose parents have not been afraid simply to love them, to play with them, to praise their work unstintingly, to take their sides against the limiting, restricting, prohibitive teachers they have had. These parents may have given lip service to the restrictive clichés of child-rearing and education, just as their inner-motivated children may have expressed the "normal" hatred of school. But if you see these parents and their children alone at home, interacting with each other in mutual love and respect, you see that they subscribe not to the clichés, but to their own humanism, strengthened in their togetherness. And you understand why the youngsters are so shining and so effective in school. Clearly their lives have meaning, instilled by the respect and comradeship of their parents and sustained by a continued alliance with them. Everything the youngsters do, including schoolwork, has meaning, and they cannot help deriving maximal benefit from it. No, these parents are not rare, and these children are not rare. But there could be more of them, filling the classrooms with eager energy and love of learning.

Developmental freedom is promoted when parents acknowledge their children's humanity and when they offer the children the opportunity to make choices. The formula applies to anyone with influence over others—foremen, teachers, therapists, friends—and it is a good formula: it works.

Listen to a college senior: "You know, I had about three classes in college where I really learned something. Freshman psychology, and anthropology when I was a sophomore, and this English class in modern novels now. You know why? Because the profs in those classes liked me and listened to me. Or at least I thought they did, and that's what counts. I wasn't some freshman goon or some dumb peasant to them, and they didn't think teaching was a big waste of time when they could have been doing their crummy research. Man, I worked in those classes, and I learned! I realized in Anthro that the reason I was pulling an *A* was because I'd decided to. Somehow in those classes I felt as if I could decide whether to study or not, whether to do outside reading I didn't *have* to do or not. And I always decided to be a student when I felt that it was valuable to the prof to have me be a student."

The student in his realm is saying the same thing as the ex-delinquent is saying in his: "The first person in the world who ever seemed to take an interest in me, and to like me, was my probation officer. He was a great guy, and I didn't know there were any great guys in the world. He told me that I could choose whether or not to steal any more cars, and I knew he was right. I'd never thought adults were ever right before, either."

A woman in a research project investigating successful marriages reflects to the investigators: "Why ·is our marriage a happy one? Mostly because of Larry. He's a happy man, and his parents were happy, and sometimes I think he doesn't even know how *not* to be happy. Not for very long, anyhow. It's fun living with him, and it makes me happy. I've been thinking, though, while I said that. I could— oh, begrudge his happiness. Some women I know would. And do. But I honestly don't. I think I make Larry happy, too. I always felt, even as a girl, that I could make a man happy. My father let me know that, every day of his life. Why, he'd look happy if I just walked in the room where he was. He was a quiet man, but I knew he loved me and was proud of me, even when I was such a brat in junior high. It didn't take me very long even then, though, to decide that I was being a brat and to cut it out. I wanted that heavenly feeling of making Dad happy more than anything else."

The formula acknowledging a child's humanity, and allowing him freedom of choice commensurate with his age, works. There is a hitch in it, however, and it comes from the authority's view of himself as an authority. It is not easy for many people to accept with assurance the influence they have over others. To be able to influence a child, a student, a probationer, an employee, a friend, one must feel confident of one's own authority, the reality and the impact of one's influence. "He never listens to me!" "One word from me, and she does as she pleases!" "That damn kid has no respect for me!" "I can't control my classes!" "They don't pay any *attention* to me!" "I took Johnny to the police station and asked the sergeant to give him a good talking-to. Maybe he'll listen to *him*." "I asked the doctor to straighten JoAnn out. I know *I* can't."

These are the wails of those who, in despair and self-depreciation, have waived their influence, abdicated from their authority, denied their own importance, devalued themselves. A person cannot acknowledge the humanity of another person until he has first acknowledged his own.

The essential first step in exerting benign and growth-inducing influence over another person is to accept and to be thankful for the fact that one has influence and can use it wisely. To deny or to relinquish one's own authority is to affirm one's uselessness—and to convince the other person that there is no value in paying attention to you.

Disobedience, disrespect, coldness, inattentiveness, laziness—these are the terms we use in describing youngsters with whom we feel, sickeningly, guiltily, we have failed. We need not have to plead guilty or to admit failure—or even to conceive of failure—if we look first at ourselves and wonder if perhaps such terms as "fearful," "inadequate," "ineffective," and "unconfident" might not apply to us.

The girl who says, "I know all my friends are getting married. Half of them already are. But I know I'm not ready to yet. I'd have to call Mother every time the baby cried—I don't know anything about being a wife yet," and the young man who says, "Hell, I don't even know how to take care of myself, much less anyone else. I'd be the worst flop of all time as a husband, and I wouldn't wish myself as a father on anyone," are realistic and wise young people. They recognize that it takes responsibility and self-respect to assume real adulthood, real authority, and they know they have yet to reach that point. They, too, are acknowledging themselves, and they are making important decisions. They were acknowledged by their parents in earlier years, or they could not be so honest now. Each of them will attain real adulthood, because they have just made an important step toward it, and the step is a solid one. They cannot backtrack now.

It is not defeatism or neuroticism to acknowledge oneself negatively, as these young people have just done. They have taken the first step of understanding their apparent inability to influence another person and have met it appropriately. It is too hard to do for some, who would rather place blame and responsibility elsewhere. It is too easy to do for some, who do have neurotic self-blaming attitudes already well established. But for most, it is rewarding and growth-inducing to be able to admit, not proudly, but not ashamedly, either, that to be human is also to err. This admission is not enough: its corollary is that to be human is to be able to choose, and to change. We grow, Frankl says, according to our interpretation of our selves. If we interpret ourselves as *human*, with all this implies for growth, change, betterment, expansion, and wisdom, then we can allow our young to grow as well.

To be human is to be unlimited. If we limit ourselves to one or two modes of behavior, one or two social or parental roles, we almost automatically limit other people, too, thus crippling them. "Husbands should or should not do this or that. Priests should . . . psychiatrists should . . . children should . . ."

The human, free life is not bounded by roles and conventions and taboos but by the self-determined restrictions and inhibitions that smooth our relationships with others. And even these are ignored when the relationship is so close, so intimate, that honest freedom is demanded if it is to continue its closeness and intimacy.

Developmental freedom does not apply just to the young. It applies to us.

XIV:
And They Began to Be Merry

It is in the application and the experiencing of developmental freedom that authenticity is born. It has already been said that the authentic parent allows developmental freedom in his children, and that the authentic child is one who has experienced and immeasurably profited from such freedom. It has also been said that developmental freedom is that happy circumstance in which a child is most able to be himself, unshackled by artificial restraints, unburdened with his parents' conflicts. When a child is honored and loved, when he is seen for himself, not as an extension of anyone else, not a validation of another's worth, then that child—every child—is authentic. He is honest, he is open, he is joyous. He brings much pleasure to those around him. He will grow into a rich adulthood. He will become an adult with confidence in himself, respect for himself, pride in himself. He will value others similarly and will enrich their lives with his love for them. He will truly honor his father and mother, and more important, he will honestly like them. His affection for his parents will not be based upon obligations, but upon love, and their autumn days will be warmed and given meaning by this love.

There is no parent who has not at one time or another, musingly or anxiously, asked himself how his child will feel about him twenty years, thirty years from now. "Will he scorn me?" "Will he come to see me?" "Will he love me?" "Will he be disappointed in me?" "Will he hold against me the things I do now?" "Will he remember . . . ?" "Will he hate . . . ?" "Will he appreciate . . . ?" "Will he understand . . . ?"

These are important questions, for they give a kind of perspective to our daily contacts with a child that may allow us a little more wisdom in discriminating between those things that are really important and those that had much better be ignored. They need not, and should not, interfere with the spontaneous everyday, here and now interaction with a child that more than anything—any guidebook or list of rules of child-rearing—promotes his healthy growth. They are background questions, or musings, pondered at night or away from the child, and they can refresh a parent who may be overly beleaguered, for the time being, with the all too often strident here and now. They can also, of course, increase parental anxiety and thereby add an unfortunate new dimension of strain in the next encounter with the child.

This seeming contradiction between pondering the

future—but not *too* much, because it may make the parent anxious and the child tense—and reacting to a child *now,* forgetting the past and having confidence that the future will take care of itself, may seem to strain the credibility of existential psychology. It may be less strained if you could hear the child say, some years later, "Look, Dad: I don't care *what* I was like when I was a kid, and I don't care what you were like, either. I want to know where we stand with each other *right now!* And besides, I really need to learn about myself. If I don't find out who I am, I'll *never* find out what to do with myself after college. Or even *in* college. Understand, Dad? Who I *am.* Not who I was, or who I'm going to be. But I need some help. I can't do it by myself. Or I don't know how. I need . . . *feedback.* I need to know what you're thinking about me now. It's really important to me. Can you tell me?"

You can be stopped by this impassioned question as you are struck by its reality. It's a hard question— "Can you tell me?"—because it forces you to answer it in its own terms. Now you have to look at your son, at your daughter, as a seeking, growing individual. And you've always seen him or her before as a child— as *your* child. Now he forces you, now she insists, legitimately, that you react to him, to her, as his own man, as her own woman. It's not easy to do. But if you can do it—if you can see, and respond to, this young man or woman without memories of the past, especially without disappointing ones, and without your own hopes for their futures, then you will help. You will have improved your relationship with your child immeasurably. And you will have taken a step in your own growth that will make you not just a better father, but a far better person.

It is, in other words, important to realize—and it's not difficult if you'll just apply such apparently contradictory dicta to your own life and to your child's— that existentialism by its nature takes account of the infinite complexity, of the manifold contradictions, of life itself. It is more respectful of life, and it is much more realistic, to say that a parent's relationship with his child exists on many levels simultaneously, and that these levels aren't even the same at any two moments in time. This is not an evasion; it is an acknowledgment of the child and of the parent as complicated, fascinating people to be honored and not to be reduced to the level of machines. One does not raise a child by following a recipe; one does not become a real person by automation; one cannot be programmed toward a better life. Existentialism says, Accept this complexity! Rejoice in it, for it is the price and the reward of your humanity. You will end up liking your child and yourself a lot more than if you try to order and discipline his life and yours according to some scheme that denies full, complex humanity to either of you. You, the parent, deserve every bit as much respect, as much acknowledgment, as your child. The relationship between you would be pathologically unbalanced if mutual respect did not exist, for in addition to being your child's mentor and teacher and model and guide, you are a person. To limit this basic reality of yourself is, to the extent you limit it, to deprive your child of that much of your reality. He needs all of you, in all your complexity, and at all your ever-changing levels, even as he needs his own complexity and his own even more rapidly changing levels of development, acknowledged and accepted by you.

"I was living a lie before my divorce," a young mother says. "I didn't love my husband, and he didn't love me. We stayed together for the children's sake, and because my folks would *die* if their precious daughter got a divorce, and because Hal would be crucified at work if he got one—he wouldn't last a day with that firm after the news broke.

"But since the divorce, after we finally saw the lie for what it was, and when we put things in perspective, do you know what happened? We both turned into real people. Honest people. Little Mike, who'd been flunking everything from Handwriting to Physical Education in his misery at our coldness, and his guilt, and everything else, is on the honor roll! And he's a happy boy! Hal is marvelous with him on their weekends, and I'm marvelous with him the rest of the time.

"Hal and I like ourselves now, because we are

being honest. We still don't like each other very much, and that's too bad. But that's how it is. But we like Mike, and he likes both of us now. The poor kid, he hates our being divorced, and he can't help but be happy about it, too. I just hope that Hal and I can help him see that both feelings are O.K., that it's not really the bind he thinks it is. We're trying. I think we'll make it: he's a great kid."

These parents are using the only "rules" in dealing with their child that are realistic: honesty, first with themselves and with each other; and trust, in themselves and in the boy, that they'll all be able to survive. These may seem unsatisfactory, too abstract, maybe applicable to Mike and his parents, but what about Susan, whose parents can't communicate at all? What about Teddy, whose father left the state and never even sends him a birthday card? What about Louise, whose new daddy moved in right away and started making her mother cry every night?

Honesty and trust are indeed abstract concepts, but we have seen how immediately and satisfactorily they can be applied if the parents themselves are authentic people. The withdrawn, uncommunicative parent is not authentic, nor is the deserting father, nor the masochistic mother, and it is unrealistic to expect honest behavior from them with respect to their children. They haven't found it possible to be honest with themselves yet, and honesty is not a trait that can be put on, like the "sincerity" of the glib and adroit salesman. It may fool the customer, but it won't fool a child.

But if the hallmarks of developmental freedom— honesty and trust—don't work with the children of inauthentic parents, even less fruitful will be the attempted application of more simplistic child-rearing techniques.

"How do I get my child to eat his meat and vegetables?"

"Give him a little taste of dessert first, so he'll know what his reward will be after he finishes his meal."

(But Johnny, seeing through the trick, wolfed the dessert and announced he was full.)

"How can I make Frances do her homework?"

"Tell her that for two hours every evening after supper she's to be in her room. You can't make her study, but you can enforce time to do it in."

(But Frances, testing her parents' liberalism, spent her two enforced hours on the telephone every night.)

"How do I keep Stanley from teasing the baby?"

"Tell him it's *his* baby, too. He's jealous, of course, and he needs to feel like a responsible and valued member of the family."

(But Stanley said, "If she's mine, I can do what I want," and redoubled his teasing.)

"Linda stole a lipstick from the department store. How do I handle this?"

"Make her return it to the manager herself. It will help her learn consequences and responsibility."

(But Linda, rather than face the manager, jumped out of the moving car on the way to the store and came very close to being killed.)

"Mark cries and screams every night, and I have to rock him to sleep. I'm going crazy!"

"Let him cry it out. He has come to associate crying with being comforted, and the association has to be broken."

(Finally, Mark did stop crying at night. But a strange lethargy seemed to possess him, and he caught one cold after another for an entire year.)

Each of these suggestions is "good" psychology in that it is grounded in experimental evidence and consistent with theories of experimental psychology. Each has been given to anxious parents countless times by countless physicians, psychiatrists, and psychologists (including the author). Each, for that matter, has "worked"—with some children, under certain circumstances. But the fact that they are far from successful with many if not most children and, indeed, frequently backfire, making the original problem even worse, ought to make us think heavy thoughts about the efficacy of such counsel. We must question the theories and even the experimental evidence on which the theories are based. We must take a further step, as the existentialists do, and question whether *any* counsel, even that future counsel based upon some yet to be discovered "perfect" theory of personality, should be followed. It seems most unlikely that any theory of personality can possibly encompass the infinite variety of human personalities, not to mention the interrelationships among different personalities. A slavish, or even a casual, adherence to the tenets of any theory, especially when the theories are as clearly inadequate as they are at this stage of psychology's knowledge, would seem inappropriate, misleading, and very possibly dangerous. *If we are to be authentic persons and if our children are to be authentic, we must somehow abandon, cast aside, transcend our need to be told what to do and how to do it!*

The authoritarian viewpoint is strong in our age of anxiety, and we are all too willing participants in it. Our children sense our own indecisiveness, our feelings of inadequacy, our reluctance to make genuine decisions based upon our own personal knowledge and opinions. They hear endlessly, "Ask your father," "Ask the doctor," "Ask the priest," and their growing doubts and disrespect for us are gradually cemented into doubts as to their own strength, their own decisiveness.

It is not easy to transcend an authoritarian back-ground. We envy people whose parents were self-sufficient and who encouraged them to be self-sufficient, for we see in their every action the proud and graceful freedom with which they conduct their lives and their affairs. We may sometimes wonder if these independent persons are not a race apart, espe-cially favored in some way, so impossible does it seem for us to behave in their decisive, confident ways. Sometimes we even feel alien to them; we hate them for their self-sufficiency, and we call them names—"conceited," "egg head," "show off," and so on—for we cannot bear the comparison with our own in-effectual selves. Such resentment is an unfortunate waste of energy, for the energy could just as well be expended in the direction of freeing ourselves from submissiveness to authority and becoming our own authorities. The first sentence of William Schutz's *Joy: Expanding Human Awareness* is, "If there is one statement true of every living person it must be this: he hasn't achieved his full potential."

A good part of this unfulfilled potential in each of us is Authority. We may deny it, we may feel un-worthy of it, we may fear it. But we have it. We are human; we have experienced life; we have developed, more deeply than we think, attitudes and opinions about life and people; and these attitudes and opin-ions are worthwhile. Some of them may be preju-diced, or ignorant, or mere hand-me-downs from our parents—but only some of them. We can discriminate these from our *own*, our personal ideas which came from ourselves, not from society or parents. It is these opinions, our own, that came from our own clear-eyed experience, regardless of what others may have told us, that constitute our authority. We must pay attention to them. We must articulate them, express them, and we must communicate them to our children. Our children will thereupon listen, for they know that what we are now saying is important, and they will truly respect us all our lives. Their respect is not the blind dependence of the authority-dominated personality, who asks, out of his feeling of incompetence, to be led and to be directed. Rather, it is the respect that one strong man holds for another, the intimate admiration that flows from identification ("I know why he's fighting, because I'm fighting for the same thing") and equalitarian affection. We can never really like people toward whom we feel either superior or inferior. We envy them, or despise them, and the thought of an intimate, affectionate relationship with them is inconceivable. We want our children truly to like us, not just submit to us or worship us. Our autumn years will be richer with this affection.

Those wise suggestions—those formulas for the finicky eater, the reluctant scholar, the sadistic big brother, the shoplifter, the "spoiled" baby—why don't they work? It is not enough to say that they don't take individual differences into account, or that they don't allow for the unstated feelings that may long have existed between child and parent or between child and society. It is not enough to say that they are based upon mechanomorphic theories that assume machine-like (or white-ratlike) behavior from human beings and are therefore doomed to be incomplete. Human beings are not machines, nor do they react mechanically and predictably to what is said or done to them.

The chief reason such counsel cannot be relied upon is that it denies humanity to the child; it ignores his impelling, driving, acute sense of self. It attends "scientifically" to his reaction patterns, his responses, and to the interplay between stimulus and response. But it pays no attention at all to the feeling, evaluating, choosing (and often angry, unhappy, and conflicted) child himself. It insults him. It sadly fails to understand him in any but the most contemptuous, patronizing sense. It is literally inhuman counsel, for it fails to acknowledge the child's humanity. It is bad counsel also in that it calls for mechanical behavior on the part of the parent: Push this button, and the machine will do such and such. Thus the parent is dehumanized too, and gradually, then rapidly, a system of stimulus and response, usually unsuccessful, is set up between parent and child, which is a frustratingly poor substitute for the natural, spontaneous interplay of mutual respect and love that leads to mature humanity for both.

"What do I do . . . ?" and "How do I handle . . . ?" are dangerous questions, dehumanizing questions, for they rend the fragile bond of spontaneity between two people and dissolve it, if carried on long enough, in the acid sterility of a mechanical relationship. "I love my mother, but I don't *like* her . . ." I love my child, but I can't stand him . . ." are the pathetic voicings that can represent the beginning of the end of true affection.

It should not be disheartening to the concerned parent that there can be no rules of child-rearing. Quite the opposite is the case: once a parent sees that his positive, natural, spontaneous reactions to his child—those reactions that are born of genuine love and respect—result in similarly loving behavior from the child, and once he sees that they stimulate and develop the child's normal and natural wish to please the parent, such that there is no room for defiance or testing limits, then, in his security, in his casting aside of anxiety, the parent is fulfilled as a parent. He sees that he is doing, on his own, a good job; and there is no more rewarding job in the world than that of a parent. There is no greater satisfaction than that which comes from doing something creative and joyous independently, instead of doing something one is bidden, or told, or advised to do. The joy of living is a happy by-product of one's humanity put to work. There can be no limits placed upon a parent's, or a child's, humanity if either is to experience fully and consistently this joy.

There are no rules, for they interfere with human reactions and interactions. Yet the humanistic approach, though it may lack structure or external order, is not without solidity. Indeed, it creates a solidity, a security of basic personality in the child— and in the parent—that lasts far longer than any chain of conditioned responses, any series of associations however felicitously reinforced: it lasts for life. We may be able to examine this solidity.

A three-month-old baby becomes distressed at his 6 P.M. feeding. His mother is tense. She's been at the hairdresser's most of the day in preparation for an important dinner party that night. She is late, and the baby seems—wouldn't you know!—unaccountably slow and finicky tonight. She finally gets most of the bottle and the rice cereal down and plops the baby in his crib. He begins to scream, losing his entire meal in the process. The mother curses, runs to the door to let the baby-sitter in, prepares another bottle and asks the baby-sitter to feed the baby while she dresses. Her husband points out that they're going to be late and that they can't be late. She takes a fast shower, dresses hurriedly, and sits at her dressing table to put on her make-up. The baby has been quiet for a while, but now he begins to cry again. The mother forces herself to stop and think a moment. She knows the baby-sitter: a nice girl, but strong-minded, with all the opinionatedness of a sixteen-year-old. The mother knows the girl will let the baby cry it out even if she is asked to rock him, for she has made it clear on previous jobs that she thinks the baby is spoiled. The baby's crying will not bother her. It's not *her* baby, and the television or the stereo or the telephone conversation will effectively drown out the noise.

The mother knows she may be making too much of this one evening. After all, the baby has eaten and slept wonderfully well ever since birth, and one night's discomfort, distress, and possible indigestion aren't going to make that much difference. She'll see to it that things won't be tense and upset tomorrow. But *might* one night make a difference? Might this unfortunate evening be the start of a three months' colic siege, during which time *every* night will be tense and sleepless for everyone in the family? She makes a decision: "I don't know, but I'm not going to take a chance."

She goes to the nursery, picks up the baby, and calls to her husband. "Dear, you go on ahead and make my excuses. I'm going to rock the baby to sleep, and then I'll call a taxi and join you. I'll get something to eat here, so don't worry."

Her husband, who has occasionally wondered if she doesn't mollycoddle the baby too much, starts to protest, but seeing her determination, stops. He feels the flickering of admiration—*he*'d never sacrifice a good dinner—and deals with the situation by kissing her and deciding that if she's not there by nine he'll come home and they'll have the evening together. The baby stops crying at this moment, and the mother smiles. "It won't be long, and it'll be good for me, too. Ask Mary Ann to clean up the kitchen, and you get going. I'll be with you soon."

There is a dangerous sequence of ills in many a baby's first year of life: the "three-month colic," followed by allergic reactions and sometimes asthma, which can sometimes devastate an entire childhood and the father's bank account. It is a sequence almost entirely psychogenic, that is, its causes are psychological. In this case, the indigestion, "colic," can be caused by eating in times of emotional stress, whether this stress is the mother's or the child's. It doesn't matter, for in the infant's indiscriminate mind his mother and he are the same. Fortunate is the baby— and the mother and the father—whose mother approaches feeding him with calm and patience, and who, as in this case, is able to compensate at once, to the baby's benefit, for occasions when feeding has not been calm. We cannot say that this one decision, to forgo a pleasant dinner, automatically forestalled a colic-allergy-asthma sequence. It probably did not, in fact, because of the baby's previous healthy feeding habits and the likelihood of their quickly reasserting themselves after the one-time disruption. But it could have, and the mother's value system, in which her baby's comfort outweighed the dinner party, is a system firmly directed toward human values.

This is a value system not easily obtained, by the way, and certainly not easily obtained without at least a quarter-century's experience. A teen-age girl could not, and should not, be expected to make so child-oriented a decision. It is to be hoped that any teen-age girl reading this book will think long and hard before committing herself to the condition of motherhood, in which such decisions must be made almost daily.

The child from one to three years is about as active an energy system as can be found. His motility and his curiosity are boundless within whatever environment he finds himself, and he is directed by this developmental drive toward the unclean as the clean, the dangerous as the safe, the improper as the proper. His discrimination and judgment are almost nonexistent, and his enthusiasm and exploratory zeal are limitless. It is tempting, considering the child's vulnerability to danger and his parents' vulnerability to exhaustion and irritability, to lay down and attempt to make the child follow a list of "no-no's." The reasoning is logical: it will save the furniture, it may save the child, and above all, it saves wear and tear on the mother's nerves.

Such a list is much more likely, especially if it is stringently enforced, to do real violence to the curiosity and exploratory drives that, unchecked, are the bases of later enthusiasm for all kinds of learning: about things, about people, about oneself, about relationships between and among things and people and oneself. Inhibitions in learning can result directly from inhibitions in activity in these active years from one to three: the mother who curtails her two-year-old's running from room to room with gates and barricades or shouts and slaps is creating an underachiever of five years hence, but she will not accept the responsibility of having done so at that time. She will probably nag or threaten or bribe him to study, wondering audibly and frequently why he won't pay attention in school. "He could get A's if he *wanted* to," she will complain, implying that it is the child's own deficiency in drive that is responsible for his "not trying." This child did try, when he was two, to learn and investigate and explore and deduce and see and understand and take apart and break and throw and squash and everything else in the inexhaustible behavioral repertoire of two-year-olds. But he soon learned that it was wrong to do so: he got yelled at and hit and immobilized, and things were taken away from him. Now that he is seven, pretty much the same thing happens when he wonders about something. He is told not to bother his parents, or his teacher makes a cruel joke at his expense, and it all becomes very clear that learning is so potentially, if not actually, dangerous that he'd be much better off simply closing his mind to the whole process. But how fascinating learning might be, if only he felt safe!

The howls of outrage that automatically greet the use of words like "unchecked," referring to the desirability of not inhibiting children's exploratory drives, are similar to the rapturous applause given a politician's promise to restore "law and order" to the land. In both cases, condemnatory or laudatory, they reinforce the authoritarian attitude: to influence people you must wield a very strong stick, for this is the only language that they (though not I!) can understand. The parent or the politician who truly feels that he can influence others only through the practice or promise of force is sadly inauthentic. He has no faith in his children's or his constituency's abilities to govern themselves, given decent conditions in which to do so, and he makes a sad mockery of democracy.

The authentic parent is one who *of course* realizes the limitations to the word "unchecked." He obviously is not going to allow his child to play unchecked on a freeway or anywhere else where the child's lack of judgment and discrimination will place his life in danger. He will *of course*—because he values children more than objects—eliminate precious breakable things from the child's surroundings. He realizes that it is more important to help a child toward the security that is the basis for a love of learning than it is to have a houseful of unbroken *objets d'art,* and he dismisses with contempt any advice about the necessity of teaching children "respect for property." This parent knows—probably because he was so raised—that respect for property or people comes not from enforcement but from the free opportunity to experience that property and those people that deserve respect. (The inauthentic parent senses his own inauthenticity; he knows he is not really worthy of respect, so he must demand it the more stringently from his children.)

Jonathan, at thirty-two, is a happily married and very successful lawyer. He is an affectionate husband, an affectionate father to his two children, and an affectionate son to his widowed mother, who is presently visiting him and his family. He and his wife love to hear her open up and speak of her past, and they urge another glass of wine upon her. She smiles at her little grandson and tousles his hair. "Bradley reminds me so much of you when you were his age, Jon," she says. "On the go every second, in and out of everything, underneath and on top at the same time."

Bradley giggles, "How could I do that, Nana?"

"Beats me," she answers. "Your father did it, too. I guess it's a secret between fathers and sons."

"Did you ever get mad at Daddy?"

"Not usually. How can you get mad at a boy for being a boy?"

"Rickey's mother does. When he climbed up on the roof she said he was a bad boy. And licked him. She practically *killed* him."

"That makes me sad. I'm sorry for Rickey's mother."

"*I'm* sorry for Rickey!"

They all laugh, and Nana goes on. "I did get awfully mad at your daddy once, though. When he was three years old, Granddad and I took him to San Francisco. It was the first time he'd ever stayed in a hotel, and he was fascinated with the elevators."

"Oh, Lord," Jonathan interrupts. "I know what's coming."

"I'll *bet* you never forgot that," his mother says. "Anyhow, one morning while Granddad and I were still asleep in bed, your father sneaked out of the room and waited by the elevators until one stopped at our floor."

"Because he was too little to reach the button," Bradley crows, shooting his father a glance of mingled fun and competitive triumph. At least Dad wasn't *always* so big!

"Right," Nana continues. "And he rode that elevator up and down a hundred times, just loving it. Well, that wasn't so bad, but after a while he decided to investigate all the other elevators in the hotel. Including the service elevator. Where a maid, not seeing him, pushed a big serving table right over his little bare foot. By this time, his father and I were all over the hotel looking for him. We figured he'd probably head for the elevators, so we stationed ourselves by them in the lobby. But no Jonny. Granddad was just heading for the house detective to report him when what did we see, coming from the service elevator, which we hadn't thought to check, but a teary-faced little three-year-old, in his pajamas, limping toward the door leading out! I ran after him and picked him up and said, 'Where in the world do you think you're going?'

"He was a little ashamed, and I could hardly hear his answer, but he finally came out with it. 'To the hotel next door,' he said—he meant the Sir Francis Drake, which was at least three blocks away—'to see *their* elevators.' "

Bradley laughed uncontrollably for five whole minutes. Through his peals of laughter he finally was able to ask, "What did you do? Spank him?"

"Oh, heavens, no," Nana said. "He'd already been punished enough. That was a nasty bruise on his foot. Besides, it obviously didn't dampen his enthusiasm for elevators any more than a spanking would have. We got him bandaged up and washed and dressed, and then we—"

"I know," yelled Bradley. "Then you took him to the Sir Francis Drake and let him ride on *those* elevators!"

"That's right, dear. How did you know?"

"Oh, I don't know. I guess it's what Mom would have done if it was me. To get it out of my system so I wouldn't run away by myself?"

Nana looked warmly at her daughter-in-law and turned back to Brad. "Yes. And for another reason, too. Do you know what?"

"Uh, no. What?"

"To show him that riding elevators, or doing anything else, is more fun if you're with someone than if you're alone."

"Hey, that's neat. Did you learn your lesson, Dad?"

Jonathan grinned. "Haven't stepped foot on an elevator by myself ever since." He sobered and turned to his mother. "You know, Mom, that *is* how it worked. I still remember giggling at Dad holding his stomach and rolling his eyes in that elevator at the Sir Francis Drake and thinking that it *was* better with him along. And how much I loved you for not getting mad at me."

"Oh, we were mad, all right. But you did have your winning ways. No wonder you're a successful lawyer today. We never could stay mad very long."

"Mind if I call you for jury duty at my next trial?"

And so from generation to generation can flow the warm, benign patterns of openness and humor and respect and understanding that characterize the authentic family. Young Bradley is learning a lesson in the value of nonviolence that is becoming an inextricable part of him. His own children, someday, will be the better for it.

It is much easier for a parent to be gentle with his children, thus storing up within them compassion for others and delight in exploring and learning that will last all their lives, if the parent himself had been raised gently. The durability and the duration of childhood patterns are such that it is also much harder for a harshly raised parent to try to reverse the pattern with his own children. In some cases, psychotherapy is needed to help the more benign and loving patterns to emerge into consistent expression. But in all cases, even without therapy, it can be done. There will be false steps and missteps and regressions and regretted acts of impulsive violence, but the child will sense that the parent is *trying,* and he will forgive and forgive and forgive.

The years of young childhood, from around four to ten or so, may be distinguished for our purposes as years in which the quality of interpersonal relationships has as much, if not more, to do with determining authenticity or inauthenticity than any other factor. In these formative years the kinds of relationships that the child will have with others the rest of his life are being laid down and formed. If, as an adult, a person is shallow, evasive, manipulative, cruel with others—if he is cold, hostile, demanding—if he is clinging, dependent, anxious, and frightened when facing others—if he is interested, warm, compassionate, kind—if he is giving, loving, affectionate—if he is any or all of these when he is with others, the chances are high that he *learned* how to be any or all of these as a young child. He can, to be sure, unlearn them if he wishes, but it is costly and difficult—and not always completely successful.

The qualities of relating to others, the complex re-actions of man to man, the understandings and the misunderstandings, the inhibitions, the gaucheries, the embarrassments, the *faux pas,* and the intense, passionate pleasure of close communion—these are the elements of real happiness and unhappiness in our lives. When we have good relationships with others who are important to us, we are content, and our lives have meaning. We are proud of ourselves—"I can love!"—and there seems little that can defeat us.

It would seem only reasonable, then, that our chil-dren be educated in successful interpersonal relation-ships, since they are so overwhelmingly important in later happiness and success, at the critical period of early childhood when the techniques and reaction patterns involved in getting along with others are being first laid down. However, children are learning many other things then, too: multiplication and the history of their state and how to play the piano and the value of money. All these other things are appar-ently considered more important in terms of time devoted to them and the training of teachers to teach them. The training children receive in interpersonal relating is unorganized, casual, considered unimportant if not a "frill," and all too often distorted, so that what children learn is how to fear others or how to exploit them.

Many exciting psychological research studies have shown how children in modified "T-" or sensitivity groups, in which people experience and learn the rewards of spontaneous and honest reactions and interactions with each other, have learned to substitute kindness for cruelty, helpfulness for exploiting, affectionate support for name-calling, just as adults in group therapy or T-groups do. Children are savages only to the extent that adults expect them to be or force them to be.

A child with a meaningful, intimate relationship with his parents, one in which he is not ignored or got out of the way at every opportunity, will grow into an adult with close relationships with others. He may not have the chance of sensitivity training (children are already so sensitive that such a program seems superfluous), but he has the chance to talk at length with his mother and his father when he wants and needs to. The almost obsessive shift, at certain ages, from dependence upon the adult world to full-time participation in the peer culture, with complete devotion to its standards and values, often those at definite odds with the standards and values of the adult world, reflects both the child's deep need for a meaningful relationship with someone and his bleak recognition that he's not about to get one with an adult. The virtually immediate reaction of candid openness with a kind and nonmoralizing adult that many so-called rebellious children show is as sad, in a way, as the defensively suspicious, guarded reactions of a more confirmed rebel. The latter child has learned that adults are not to be trusted, and this is too bad for him, for he still needs them. But the other child is just as pathetic, for his healthy reaction shows how badly deficient in meaningful relationships his life has been.

It is an exciting experience for a psychologist to watch the progression from suspicion to openness in communication, sometimes occurring within an hour in his office. A tough, defiant girl, brought in by parents despairing of her stealing and lying, her rudeness and flippancy, her obscenity and possible drug-taking, is determined not to talk to the headshrinker. She sits in ugliness, glaring, as he begins to ask her questions and to disclose himself as a potential friend. At the end of the hour, she says, "Gol, this is fun! Can I have another appointment?" She is very pretty then, and she is so very relieved at not having to wear the heavy armor of defensiveness, at least with this one man. She has really communicated, for a whole hour, with another person; the experience is intoxicating. We can give this experience to our children all the time, not just once in their lives and, at that, paying someone else to do it.

A five-year-old girl and her father are sitting by their pool on a warm summer evening. It's past the child's bedtime, but both are reluctant to end the quiet pleasure of their communion. They are talking about the stars, and the father is describing some of the constellations. The child, with five-year-old shifting attention, asks, "Daddy, what would you do if a man from Mars came down and landed in the pool?"

"Tell me what you'd do, dear."

"Oh, guy. I'd run into the house as fast as I could. I'd be scared! Wouldn't you?"

"Well, maybe. But I think I'd pull him out of the pool first. And then, I'd probably try to talk to him, to see if we could understand each other."

"No, you wouldn't," his daughter announces flatly. "Not at first. I know what you'd do first, after you got him out of the pool."

"What?"

"You'd offer him a daiquiri."

The father's amusement at the little girl's perception of his social techniques lasted a long time. But he was surprised, ten years later, when he read a theme his then high-school daughter had written on the topic Communication: "Communication is when you can sit with your father at night and he tells you things that are interesting, and he wants to know if you understand them and how you feel. And maybe you're little and say funny things, except you don't know they're funny, and your father laughs, but not too much, because he knows you might think he's laughing at you. Like once, a long time ago, I was talking to my father by our pool . . ."

And there followed a verbatim transcript of the ten-year-old conversation, a talk in its warmth and closeness that had been treasured by the child all that time. In the beauty of communion with a child we gain much: we glimpse the depths of sensitivity the child possesses; and we get a clear-eyed, completely honest, and sometimes startling glimpse of ourselves. We cannot lose; and the child gains an appreciation of the joy of total communication with another that will make him forever intolerant of shallow contact.

In considering authenticity, we have been discussing children as isolated non-adult members of the family and almost the only offspring of their parents' love. Actually the doctrine of close interpersonal relationships as a hallmark of an authentic life is nowhere so strained, so out-and-out questionable, as in the area of sibling relationships. The television family show, in which adorable children of all ages work together in a harmony gladdening to the heart which is marred only occasionally by some cunning deviltry instantly seen through and wisely solved by an equally cunning parent, presents a model that is, to say the least, hard to follow. The rasp of children's bickerings and mutual accusations seems to destroy parental patience far more than their many cooperative and amicable moments with each other can restore it. In a conference on increasing parental effectiveness held by the American Association for Humanistic Psychology in San Francisco in August 1968, parents indicated that problems involving sibling rivalry were more numerous, more irritating, and less easily dealt with than any other—and this in days of problems such as marijuana smoking by the very young that would seem much more serious!

The two problems do, however, present quite different levels of concern, and it is not appropriate to compare them. Most parents can deal, for better or worse, wisely or foolishly, with "real" problems, the serious ones, in which right and wrong are more easily distinguished, whether in terms of the child's health and safety or societal dicta. But in the seemingly endless war between and among children in the same family that so often prevails, the parent is harassed not only by the sheer volume and discordance of the battles but also by his inability to know precisely who's right and who's wrong; who the transgressor, who the victim; where, in short, justice really lies. Even the worst-written, most unrealistic television script at least gives a viewer most if not all sides of a given situation; and this, plus the still-flourishing tendency of writers to stereotype their characters—most are either good guys or bad guys—makes it very easy to solve problems tranquilly on the tube. In the meantime, the television room reverberates with the harsh clamor of children screaming at each other, the dinner goes down indigestibly as the children flout the theoretical therapy of a relaxed meal. No wonder the distress of sibling rivalry is the hardest to bear!

There is another reason, a far more important one, that explains the anxiety of parents in trying to deal with rivalrous behavior among their children. It is a reason not often articulated or even recognized: it is that sibling rivalry is *in fact* a symptom of real unhappiness among children, even of psychological disturbance; and this is a fact few parents wish to acknowledge. We therefore are quick with our reassurances and rationalizations to each other: "It's perfectly normal. All children squabble. Why, I worry when they're *not* fighting. It builds character and healthy aggressiveness. It's a competitive world, and they might as well learn it now." Et cetera, et cetera, et cetera.

There is probably no relationship, even the most cloistered, in which some competitive elements do not exist. Siblings are not the only rivals, it hardly needs to be pointed out; marital relationships are notably,

if unconsciously, rivalrous, and one of the leading
psychological causes of divorce is just this: that each
partner feels somehow put down by the other in the
contest of who is to be tops, who is to prevail, who is
to be ascendant, who descendant in their parallel—
but, sad to say, infrequently intertwining—quest for
identity and security. It may be that at least two relatively contemporary phenomena—communal marriages and the apparent desexualization of hippy
youth, where behavioral and physical distinctions
between the sexes are blurred virtually to the vanish-
ing point—are reactions to sensitive people's awareness of the destructive aspects of such competition. It
is probably very safe to say that most hippies have
grown up in an atmosphere of parental bickering,
"parental rivalry," and that they, unlike their more
stolid siblings, have elected to have none of it themselves. These youngsters have decided that the war
between siblings and the war between the sexes have
been fought long enough, and have finally determined to protect themselves from the corrosion of
vicious competition. The war between the generations
rages.

It may also be that in abandoning traditional sex
roles, garb, behavior, and attitudes that have so long
contributed to suspicion, distrust, uneasiness, and discomfort between the sexes—and ultimately to battles
and divorce—these sexually indistinguishable young

people are forging much stronger sexual identities than their parents ever had. The incidence of perversions and sexual unresponsiveness among people raised in traditional patterns of sex-typing is, we know, high enough. It may become even higher among those who today are dressing and doing their hair with supreme disregard for the "rules" of sex-typing, who are experimenting in their teens with group living, with homosexuality as well as heterosexuality, with compassion and trust and mutual dependence between the sexes at a far earlier age than ever before. And again, it may not. That conscious rejection of traditional sex-typing might prove a breakthrough to much firmer sexual identification in adulthood, where men are thoroughly and satisfyingly masculine, and women happily feminine, is a hypothesis not to be scorned automatically. Our identities in whatever area are formed, after all, only on the basis of searching and experimenting and thinking about them. If we have not been allowed to search and experiment and think but instead have been forced into expected roles by others—"Little boys don't cry," "Little girls don't get dirty"*—as so many of the present generation of parents have been,

---

* A recent television commercial shows a housewife, extolling the virtues of some detergent, holding a gleamingly white dress and saying, regarding her daughter's messiness, "Why, Jenny is as *bad* as the boys!" (Italics are mine.) Apparently even boys shouldn't get dirty any more.

then it is not surprising that our identities have proved to be shallow and quickly susceptible to breakdown.

The communal marriage rite is not so clearly a reaction against the strife of monogamous marriages, at least in its stated purpose, which is to provide men and woman the fulfillment of their many and often disparate needs which, they say, only one spouse could not begin to provide. The statistics on adultery, and more tellingly, the *lack* of statistics on adultery, an increasingly accepted way of life among all social classes and in all parts of the country, indicate most clearly and emphatically the truth of the premise that monogamy is for many an impossible way of life. Whether or not it *is*, in fact, impossible, is a question not likely to be answered by the assumption that it is, with consequent "solutions" in adultery, wife-swapping, and communal marriages. The most cogent argument against these "solutions" is that invariably other people become involved in the adulterous (to whatever degree) affairs. The "best friend" is told; the wife is tipped off, frequently by the erring husband himself, in an "accidental" way of being found out. Research in communal marriages shows that a consulting psychiatrist is needed to work through the complex emotional entanglements resulting from the ménage if the commune is to remain intact. (It is not stated whether or not the psychiatrist belongs to the commune, but it is unlikely that he does.) It seems a rather forceful argument against the meaningfulness of an adulterous relationship if it cannot be sustained on its own, but must rather be dependent upon the support, or at least the knowledge, of others.

So rivalry, competition, defensiveness of one's own position, and rationalizations disguising the truth of a relationship go on, all in the presence of the knowing or suspecting or simply sensing children. We offer effective models to our children, and we have little ground for complaint when they copy us.

Imitation of parental rivalry is not, however, an explanation of sibling rivalry: it simply shows the youngsters how to express their feelings. The reason for sibling rivalry lies in the children's feeling that their selves, their precious and still precarious inner identities, their egos, have somehow been violated. It takes maturity to react to competition, and even more to react to backbiting or injustice or manipulation, with relative equanimity, with understanding or tolerance or patience. Often, of course, such controlled reactions do not represent maturity at all, but rather passivity or fear or masochism. But for the most part, justice and harmony in interpersonal relationships are probably best served by restraint, by not allowing oneself to react on the same level as that of the provoker. A childish squabble is usually irritating, but it is downright disgusting when one of the participants is an adult.

The frequency with which adults do engage in

childish bickering—with each other as well as with their children—indicates the difficulty of reaching that level of maturity at which reason can replace the first impulsive, and childlike, reaction of striking back at the same level. Under attack, or when we feel attacked, the heritage of our long childhood almost automatically asserts itself. Like our children, we feel our identities violated when we are snubbed or criticized or humiliated; and there are relatively few adults who can bear such attacks "maturely." And yet our identities, as adults, are far more secure than those of our children, even if we consider ourselves neurotic, simply because of our greater age and experience. It is not at all fair to expect a maturity and a security from children that we often fail to show ourselves. And it is doubly unfair when we consider how much more frequently children's fragile egos and identities come under attack than do ours. An overweight adult is much less often made fun of than his overweight child. And when he is, he has many more resources—joking, rationalizing, counterattacking and the like—to protect his equally vulnerable ego than has his child.

There is another similarity between the behavior of adults and children, but with an important difference in consequences, such that the child becomes more likely to exhibit the quarrelsome, ego-protective behavior we call sibling rivalry. Both adults and children tend to build their own egos, their own self-images, through disparaging and criticizing others, especially when under stress. But the adult who tears down his co-worker or her neighbor is listened to and tacitly supported in his own ego game, while the child is punished and made to feel guilty for the same tactic.

The dynamics of sibling rivalry may be seen in relative completeness: a child feels, for whatever reason, correctly or incorrectly, that he has been put down, misunderstood, treated unjustly, exploited. His young ego cannot tolerate this altogether; it becomes wounded and sometimes damaged. He voices his dismay, his pain, in the language of wounded children: whining, crying, screaming or acting-out physically. To restore his self-esteem he must seek vengeance, and we have seen how belittling or making scapegoats of others, how responding in kind can, he thinks, accomplish such restoration. After all, he has seen his parents do it often enough. He strikes out at the supposedly guilty party. (The "guilty" brother or sister is sometimes an innocent but more available and less powerful surrogate of a parent.) The scapegoat immediately strikes back with all the outrage he is capable of, which is a great deal. The possibilities, the elaborations, the hurt are limitless, and it may take eighteen or twenty years—perhaps it may never be possible—to bring peace among the brothers and sisters.

The size of the family—the number of siblings—

is most definitely a factor in the intensity of sibling rivalry, the degree of disturbance it implies, and the damage it can do. An only child has sibling rivalry problems, perhaps the most ominous of all, for his siblings exist only in fantasy, and he has not the reality of brothers and sisters against which to check out and to test his fantasies. On the other hand, he has the relatively undiluted attention of his parents, which will, if wisely applied, do much in strengthening his ego, confirming his identity, and hastening the maturity that will allow him to respond to others more appropriately than by feeding into *their* rivalries. He does not have the opportunity, no matter how many other children he may play with, to solve rivalry problems with his peers on the intimate level possible only within a family. In all, the only child comes out a loser.

The child from a very large family often seems less rivalrous than one from a much smaller one, but his apparent docility and cooperativeness may well be simply a forced acquiescence to the overwhelming number of demands made on him by his older siblings as well as his parents. He may, that is, be unable to express any feelings of wounded pride because of the overriding necessity of pulling his weight in so large a family in such a way that all can survive—as has been pointed out to him since birth. He suppresses them, becomes a "good" child—and perhaps a submissive adult. The overt expression of sibling rivalry, although irritating, is by no means a bad thing. How else can a parent become aware of his child's feelings and thereupon do something about them? And it is also clear that a child with so many siblings cannot begin to have the necessary amount of attention and ego-building time from his parents (unless, of course, they have as many servants as children) that are required for normal psychological growth. Even if he does get this attention, by demanding it, he is likely to be made to feel so guilty about the demands that the value of the parental attention is at once lost.

An exception may be noted in the fortunate case of an oldest child—she had six younger siblings—who, in her adult years, said, "I know *exactly* why it worked out so well for me. And I feel sorry for all the downtrodden people I know who spent all their child-hoods taking care of their little brothers and sisters. They're sad, now. Sad, because it seems as if they don't know how to *enjoy* things. Or maybe they never learned. But my mother *wanted* every one of her chil-dren. Sure, I had lots of jobs to do. I grew up during the Depression, and believe me, I had to work. I worked hard. But I *never* had to be a mother. My mother accepted her responsibilities, and I guess I ac-cepted mine. But they didn't overlap. She was the mother, always. Maybe that's why I enjoy my brothers and sisters so much now. Maybe that's why they like me."

Sibling rivalry, as an expression of violated self-esteem, is a valuable clue to the concerned parent that a need exists, that a developing ego needs some love and attention, and that there may well be unseen injustices in the home that require remedying. It can be minimized—though never eradicated—by thoughtful attention to each child's individuality, by downgrading or even eliminating the so-called virtues of cooperation when they are really just techniques imposed by parents for easing a too-crowded situation. The overcrowding is the parents' fault, not the child's, and he should not be expected to solve problems, particularly at the expense of his own ego development, for which he was not responsible.

The child who for the most part gets along cooperatively and affectionately with his siblings, who shares with them, who gives to them and takes from them happily—and there are many such children—is a child secure in his own identity. He is unthreatened by the others, for he knows he is valued as an individual, not just as a family member. He has not been made to feel responsible for the younger ones or obligated to obey the older ones, and there is, accordingly, none of the resentment that always accompanies too early responsibility or dependence upon arbitrary authority. His nonrivalrous behavior, his affection, and his cooperation stem from his sense of individual worth.

Up to the age of ten or so, the authentic child has

learned trust and his own value as a person; he has learned to express, safely, his curiosity and zest for life; and he has learned to value other people and to value communicating with them. In addition, of course, he has learned many other things, chiefly skills. He has learned to pay attention; he has learned about industry and endurance at tasks; he has learned a rudimentary morality. He will continue, for the rest of his life, to learn new skills and develop old ones. His cognition will expand to deal with abstractions that are merely formulas to him now, and his morality may develop to the point where he obeys rules to avoid self-condemnation.

Now, at ten, and also lasting the rest of his life, the authentic child begins the most fascinating adventure of all: the exploration and understanding of himself. He begins to test himself, alone and with others, to find where he falls short, where his talents lie, what he can do on his own, how attractive he is to others, whom he can fool, whom he can dominate, whom he loves. He spends endless hours in absorbed contemplation of himself—his dreams and fears and fantasies, his body (especially its developing sexuality), his social techniques and their success or lack of it. Above all, he contemplates his central self, that mysterious, possibly omnipotent and certainly magical, abused, misunderstood, constant—indeed, eternal—core that keeps him going and keeps him authentic.

When a child loses this compelling, fascinating sense of his central self—when he discards it, convinced of its worthlessness, or when it is forced by others' too harsh dominance into disrepair and finally, dysfunction—then he loses his authenticity. There is no center to his personality, and he is disorganized, or fragmented. He is incoherent, aimless. He is in chronic conflict, with himself and necessarily with others who try to impose direction or organization upon him.

Anyone, child or adult, must always be acutely aware of his central self if he is to have meaning and if he is to impose meaning upon his life. We can help children toward this meaningfulness, toward authenticity, toward insight, by valuing their inner selves even more—*much* more—than we value their outer selves, their manners and their speech habits and their neatness and their haircuts and their study habits and the friends they go around with.

"My husband announced at breakfast this morning that he wasn't coming home tonight unless Steve got a haircut. Now, I ask you. He didn't even say it directly to Steve. He expects me to enforce it, and I have no intention of doing so. He doesn't even *know* Steve! He hasn't had two words of pleasant conversation with him in years. All he can see is that haircut, or that *non* haircut, and all he can say is, 'You're judged by your appearance.'

"After he stomped out, Steve asked me if I didn't think Dad was being more childish than he was. I didn't say so, but the boy is right. I don't like this, either, taking his side against his father. But Steve is a good, sweet boy! He works hard, he's bright and thoughtful, and I'm very, very proud of him. Maybe he is judged by his appearances—personally, I don't think he looks bad at all, and besides, the long-hair fad will be over someday, or else everyone will have it—but I don't think *any* kid should be judged by his parents. There's no one else who will love him for what he is, not now, when he's only fifteen. If he doesn't have us to *really* know him, who does he have? No wonder kids his age join gangs or fall in love. They've got to have someone who likes *them,* not just what they look like. Well, Steve's going to have me at least, if not his father. But I wish—oh, how I wish— he could have both of us. He needs his father a lot more than he needs me right now.

"I think Fred will come home tonight. Well, of course he will. He's really not that childish. And I'll talk to him. With him. Steve will, too. We'll work it out."

An early adolescent's insight into his own workings is far from complete or even accurate. He often sees others with a clarity, even profundity, that is in no way reflected in his view of himself. He can pierce phoniness in others with deadly aim, while entertaining just as strongly the most patently false or stereotyped notions about himself. It would seem to be a developmental sequence: trust in others precedes self-trust. Understanding others precedes and is the necessary basis for understanding oneself.

"Dad talks a lot about taking responsibility, but he hasn't made a decision about anything really important for years . . . I didn't hand in that essay today because the crummy teacher didn't say I was supposed to."

"Mom's always saying how 'beautiful' sex is, but Dad slept on the couch in the living room every night last week . . . I know everything about sex, and I don't have any questions about it."

"My mother always told me to think for myself, but she divorced my father, and she's sorry she did—especially since he married that girl—just because her psychiatrist told her to. I think the psychiatrist just got all hung up on mother—he never did talk to Dad. He said it was 'unprofessional.' Well, I think *he* was unprofessional, and I hate him . . . The only reason I got busted last night was because of the kids I was with. They had bad reputations, and the cops were laying for them. *I* didn't do anything."

We can help our early teen-agers toward the imperative "Know thyself" not by pointing out critically these inconsistencies, nor by laughing at them, for such treatment tends to reinforce and strengthen them. Nor can we really answer the youngsters' unasked questions (for they are, dimly, aware of the inconsistencies) by ignoring them, figuring that in time the kids will straighten out their thinking. If we are honest with ourselves, we can see all too many such inconsistencies in our own thinking, and if time were all that mattered we would be old enough to have outgrown them. We must ask our children to look at the inconsistencies, to confront them, in a manner that lets the kids know we're on their side. This is not a role we assume as dutiful parents. If it is, the children see through it at once as simply one more adult trick, and we get nowhere. We have to *be* on their side. We have to be determined that our children will not identify with the hypocrisies and inconsistencies and "logic-tight" compartmentalized thinking that has got us into so much trouble. We must commit ourselves to honesty. This is not the false honesty that goes under the banners of "The truth hurts," or "This is for your own good"; these are rationalizations we use to punish young people out of our own thwarted needs. It is the honesty of genuine love, and it says, "Listen, you wonderful, mixed-up kid. You're saying something that doesn't make sense. Well, I love you, and I want you to see what the sense of it is, because you won't be so bitter or defensive if you do. You're right about your father [or the psychiatrist or your mother], but I don't think you've told the whole story about yourself. I don't think you *know* it yet. Tell me again, and let's see if we can learn more about you."

If we do not love our children, then we cannot help them—we can only hurt them. There is no use trying. We must simply get them somewhere else, into some home or institution where they may have a better chance of being loved, and hence helped toward self-honesty. If we do love our children, then we have already helped them along this road, and we are already reaping the benefits—among other things, by loving them more. But if we do love them, but have buried or forgotten or somehow lost this love in a complex of resentment and hurt feelings and martyrdom and outrage and disillusionment and pain and bad experiences with them, then we must most mightily bestir ourselves to recapture it. If we do not, lost love becomes no love forever, and our children face their lives alone, vulnerable, without self-understanding. They are doomed to shallowness in their relationships with others and to dishonesty and rationalization within themselves.

Recaptured love is not only possible, it is inevitable—with good will. Good will means a casting aside of past grudges, an opening of oneself to the fresh breezes of the present, an immediate, delight in coming again to know the stranger, to see him become no longer "strange" but known. It is more than forgiving, for it involves forgiving oneself as well. It is a triumphant exercise to recapture love, for it means that the adult *decides* to do it and then takes the first steps toward it, for he is the more mature. He realizes, more than the child, the dread and empty consequences of not doing it. Many young adults have experienced recaptured love when they suddenly see their parents as friends, even contemporaries, and a new-old relationship between them is kindled. It is this kind of kindling, an acting-upon of the long-withheld wishes for close contact by both parent and child, that can recapture the most deeply buried love.

"I'm fifteen now, and I haven't seen my father since I was four, when he left us. I used to cry for him, and then I hated him, and then I sort of forgot him. But now I'm hunting for him. I don't know why, but I really want to see him, just for a minute, even. I *have* to."

"When the police called, and said our John was in Juvenile Hall and we could come see him, I was hit by this awful bundle of feelings: that he'd done all the terrible things we'd always warned him about, and that we'd *forced* him into doing them by harping about them all the time. But when we got there, and

I saw him standing there, so—*young,* and looking so afraid and so ashamed—well, I forgot about that bundle, that terrible, destructive thing that stood between us, and all I wanted to do was hug him and tell him everything would be all right and take him home."

> But the father said to his servants, Bring forth the best robe and put it on him; and put a ring on his hand, and shoes on his feet:
> And bring hither the fatted calf, and kill it; and let us eat, and be merry:
> For this my son was dead, and is alive again; he was lost, and is found. And they began to be merry.
> —Luke, 15:22–24

"Dad, this war isn't *like* your war! Your war was—well, justified. This one isn't. You can't judge me by 1942 standards. This is 1969!"

"Dad, I know 'conscientious objector' is a dirty phrase to you. It would be to me, too, if I'd fought in World War II. But it's not dirty, now. It's . . . it's kind of great. It means cowardice to you, but it means real heroism to me. I'm not a hero, Dad, but I'd like to think I could be. At least, I'm going to try."

"Mother, look at your life. Three things. The guild, parties, and golf. That's all right for you: you like them. But not for me. I don't want to go to the club with you tonight, and I don't want to marry Tom, or anyone else right now. I'm going into the Peace Corps, if I can get in, and try to find out what I want to do in a place, in a . . . an environment that *means* something! How can I find anything real about myself if everything around me is phony?"

"Vic, let's break it off, shall we? I'm sorry. I like you a lot. Maybe I love you. I thought I did for a long time. But I keep thinking, maybe I just think I'm *supposed* to love you. Like we've been pushed together by other things or other people. I know darn well you've thought the same thing, so don't say anything until I'm through. I'd hate that, Vic. Thinking I was in love with you, and getting married, and everything, and then someday finding out we were . . . oh, you know, socially pressured into it . . . and all the time I wasn't even there, to know or to decide what *I* wanted. And it's even worse to think that . . . It's even worse to think that *you* might not really have anything to say about it. I don't want us to end up hating each other."

"Mom, I asked Dr. Thatcher for a prescription for birth control pills today, and he said I had to have your permission."

"Look, Dad, the only difference between me blowing pot and you going out of your mind blind-drunk

every night is that it's not hurting me, and you're killing yourself."

"No, I'm not going to church with you! You two
don't have the faintest idea what religion's all about.
You just go there to be seen and because it's good for
business and to be told how great you are and how
awful everyone else is and to put on a big show! You
just put your minds in neutral the minute you walk
in. Why don't you take off your hat, Mom? Take off
your jacket, Dad. And sit down here with me. Right
now. And I'll try to start you off on some simple
meditation. Come on, Dad, it's not funny. I'm serious.
I promise you, you'll find out what religion can really
do for you."

"Dad, Janice needs to have an abortion. We've
talked about it, and it's the only sensible thing to do.
But I need about four hundred more dollars."

"Oh, no, I don't! I don't owe you a damn thing!
I didn't ask to be born. Look, I'm not mad, and I'm not
ungrateful. But I will not let you make me feel obligated to you, or guilty. You know something? If you'd
get off that 'Honor thy father and mother' kick, I'd
honor you a lot more. *Really* honor you. We could be
friends. And you'd feel a lot better, too."

. . .

"We do not owe allegiance to a musty piece of cloth..."

—David Harris, August 21, 1968

"Don't trust anyone over thirty."

To hundreds of thousands of bewildered parents— conscientious, loving parents who have raised their sons and daughters with love and respect and freedom—the "generation gap," as revealed in the above impassioned outcries, is a cruel and confusing reality. It is a barrier between them and their late adolescent children that is unassailable enough in itself and is made even more formidable by the accouterments and symbols and behavior patterns of the substantial proportion of our youthful population that is most articulate and most active in its deliberate alienation: the bizarre costumes, the relative unreachability of a youth high on some drug, the absolute unreachability of a youth run away. It seems to these very uncomfortable, often panic-stricken parents that every value the kids have ever been exposed to is being thrown out, with nothing except license and anarchy as substitutions.

This is too hasty a conclusion, for it applies only to the inauthentic rebels, the really lost aliens, the ones who have been raised with brutality or indifference or injustice. It may well be that these youngsters are suffering from a kind of anomie, a rootlessness, possibly—as Erik Erikson suggests, a form of psychosis.

We are not here concerned with psychopathological youth,* but rather with authentic youth, most if not all of whom we heard voice their passion at the beginning of this section. It behooves us to take these youngsters very, very seriously—not only to recapture the closeness that was once ours and theirs but also to learn something from them. They often display a maturity exceeding ours in their commitments, their ideals, their values.

From a developmental standpoint, the values espoused so stridently by these young people are an essential part of the most important step of their lives, the logical consequence of their task of early adolescence: finding out about themselves. This is the search for identity, or wholeness, about which it seems appropriate to quote at some length Erik Erikson, who originated the telling phrase "identity crisis," and who has written most profoundly about it:

* Psychopathological youth can be easily distinguished. It voices its "philosophy" in empty phrases, characterized almost exclusively by clichés such as "out of sight" and "Wow!" and it in no way allows itself to reveal itself as human. These tragic young people are terribly afraid of their humanity. They have found a uniformed substitute for it. They do not know, yet, that the substitute—the uniforms, the empty, inhuman "philosophy" that denies their insecurities, that seems to answer their questions—will last only as long as there are others to articulate it, and to agree, with them. When they are alone, these youths suffer much more than we know.

The end of childhood seems to me the . . . crisis of wholeness. Young people must become whole people in their own right, and this during a developmental stage characterized by a diversity of changes in physical growth, genital maturation, and social awareness. The wholeness to be achieved at this stage I have called a *sense of inner identity*. The young person, in order to experience wholeness, must feel a progressive continuity between that which he has come to be during the long years of childhood and that which he promises to become in the anticipated future; between that which he conceives himself to be and that which he perceives others to see in him and to expect of him. Individually speaking, identity includes, but is more than, the sum of all the successive identifications of those earlier years when the child wanted to be, and often was forced to become, like the people he depended on. Identity is a unique product, which now meets a crisis to be solved only in new identifications with age mates and with leader figures outside of the family. The search for a new and yet reliable identity can perhaps best be seen in the persistent adolescent endeavor to define, overdefine, and redefine themselves and each other in often ruthless comparison, while a search for reliable alignments can be recognized in the restless testing of the newest in possibilities and the oldest in values.

The "newest in possibilities and the oldest in values" are the humanistic, love-centered values these authentic young people are seeking and testing, and we are sadly deceiving ourselves if we consider these values to be thrown aside by anarchistic youth. We are not being fair to our youth if we deny them the opportunity to test these values, and we are not being realistic if we deny them contemporary means and methods of testing them. They are doing exactly the same things we did, and our parents did, and theirs; the form, of course, is different, just as our experimentation in identity-formation was different in form from that of our parents. True, the forms chosen by today's youth are *very* different, perhaps shockingly so; but we cannot deny that every aspect of their lives today is very different from ours when we were their age.

It is an important thesis of this book that authenticity, which might here be redefined as a realistic awareness of one's identity (the degree of awareness, of course, being a function of the developmental level one has reached), is characterized among other things by the ability to make intelligent decisions. It follows, then, that anything which impairs decision-making—the reference here is specifically to drugs—drugs that are soporific, psychedelic, stimulating, intoxicating, or tranquilizing—therefore impairs authenticity. It may be in some ways appropriate for some youngsters and with some drugs to experiment, in order to find out for themselves the essential aridity of such experience. But clinical experience indicates that the truly authentic young person has no need for such experimentation. He cannot make legitimate choices while his mind is beclouded or hyperstimulated, and he knows he would resent such a crippling. Besides, his "trips" come from talking and skiing and surfing and loving and working—from stretching his muscles, his emotions, and his mind. Exercise of any of these is active, not passive. We do not become strong, loving, or educated by sitting back and letting it happen—it won't. The "expansion" attributed to drugs is illusory and, at best, transient. It seems not to have any degree of permanency in terms of heightened awareness, much less personality change for the better. From a psychological point of view, the continued use of drugs must be considered inauthentic and regressive, just as the use of alcohol and tranquilizers by the parents of youthful drug-takers is, more often than not, equally inauthentic and regressive. A youngster who trips on LSD is saying, just as a middle-aged alcoholic and a hypochondriacal pill-swallower are saying, "There's something missing in my life. I don't want to know what it is, because if I do (and deeply, I do know), I'll probably not be able to get it. So let's try something else that might make up for it, or, more likely, help me forget what it is I really want."

When we can listen to what these people are really saying, when we can transcend our impulses to punish, penalize, or imprison them, then, in the very act of nonpunitive listening, we help them. And thereby we become authentic ourselves.

Authenticity and the joy of living are not goals in themselves. Love, contrary to the dreams of many a youth, is not a goal in itself. The person, youth or adult, who says he is hunting for love is not very likely to find it. Love is an abstraction, and we do not hunt for abstractions but rather for specifics. Love comes from involvement, from living with a person and sharing with him and building something with him. Love does not spring full-blown from a chance encounter. Love cannot exist at the beginning of a relationship. "Love at first sight" is a strictly Hollywood invention and cannot play a part in the lives of real people. Love is a by-product of involvement.

The so-called love that starts young people off together is a mixture of physical attraction and practicality and social pressure and inner pressures. If they trust each other enough, and if they are mature and patient and not unduly narcissistic, then true love will develop as they work and share and communicate and sleep with each other. Even the relationship between a mother and her baby is not truly love at the beginning. It too grows, with caring and feeding and interacting with each other to the point, as in a marriage, where each enriches the other.

232

Trust, openness, honesty, and communication are the first steps—with our children as with our wives and husbands. From these, love grows. As love grows, and our ability to love grows, so does authenticity grow.

XV:
A Different Beauty

We spend some time talking with a child, and as he leaves he turns to us and smiles. It is a smile of love and gratitude. It is a reflection of the child's sunny and affectionate self. It is sheer beauty, and it warms us.

At a high school football game we watch the youthful musicians in the band, the cheerleaders, the players. There is an intensity in them, a focused energy, a devotion to their job so compelling that our eyes suddenly mist, and our throats catch, and we experience a different beauty, but one just as durable and just as warming.

There is beauty, too, in a child's facing his fear. He may succumb to it; he may overcome it; he may bluff his way through it. But there is always courage in the moment of confrontation with fear, and courage is awesome and beautiful to look upon.

The jeweled moments of beauty a child gives us are endless and cumulative. The experience of beauty, even if we catch only one of these moments in an hour, or a day, of a child's life, is the reward of being a parent—or a teacher, or a playground supervisor. It is the justification, the validation, the softening of obligatory into willing responsibility. To experience a child's joy, or love, or courage is not a vicarious reward: it is a deeply enriching personal and immediate experience that makes us not only better parents and teachers and playground supervisors, but most of all, makes us better persons.

To be an authentic parent is to appreciate the beauty of children and thereby to become beautiful oneself.

We cannot clearly appreciate a child's many moments of beauty if he is away, especially if we sink into a chair with a cup of coffee and say, for the benefit of our equally inauthentic neighbor, "Thank God for school. I'll have a few hours of peace and quiet at least."

We cannot appreciate these many beauties if we don't create time to see them and to savor them. In any event, we will not see them if we do not look for them, or if we dismiss them as either inconsequential or merely "cute." We especially will not see them if we interpret them in negative, or hostile, or martyred terms.

We can see beauty in our children genuinely, even objectively, only if we allow our real feelings to come to full awareness. We need not fear "spoiling" our children by delighting in them. We will not make them monsters of grabbing brattiness by indulging them. We will not create clingingly dependent adults by giving time, ungrudged, to them when they are young.

We want to give these gifts to our children. There are no parents, regardless of the pressure on them, who cannot give as unstintingly as necessary, and more, if they will only hold discourse with themselves and find these real wishes, viable and good, though buried perhaps under layers of myth and should-nots. The parents who deeply want to give, without reservations or conditions, to their children—even as they themselves would want to be given to—but who are constrained from doing so by their own parents' example or what the neighbors might say—may profit from reading anthropology to see the happy results of taboo-free joy in children expressed by more primitive mothers. They may need to cut down on the drugs, the pills, the projects, the busy activities that are said to be therapeutic but which serve only to deaden, to dull, or to deflect us from the fresh appreciation of our children. A clear-eyed response to beauty will fill us with a thrill for life—our own as well as our child's—that no pill, no bridge game, no good works will ever equal.

To unearth our true feelings takes time and insight and honesty. To act upon them takes courage and patience (for a child previously stunted will take a long time testing and regressing until he is sure that the abundance he now feels before him is genuine and will not shortly and arbitrarily be cut off). But the result is a different beauty, authenticity, a full and warming pride in oneself and growing and mutual love between oneself and one's child.

It has been said earlier that every child is authentic. So, too, is every parent, potentially. If he is not now authentic, he can become so by allowing his natural love for his child to grow unstinted by false values, unhampered by formulas and pat answers. Just as "happiness" is not an end in itself but rather a by-product of aware living, so also is authenticity a growing and enriching by-product of the wished-for giving to, respecting, appreciating, and unconditionally loving a child. Every parent has within himself the capacity to bring these wishes, these feelings, to life.

Bibliography

Anderson, J. E. "Personality Organization in Children," *American Psychologist*, 1948, III, 409–16.

Barrett, William. *Irrational Man: A Study in Existential Philosophy*. New York: Anchor Books, 1962.

Bayley, Nancy. "Some Increasing Parent-Child Similarities During the Growth of Children," *Journal of Educational Psychology*, 1954, XLV, 1–21.

Bugental, J. F. T. *The Search for Authenticity*. New York: Holt, Rinehart and Winston, Inc., 1965.

Bugental, J. F. T. *Challenges of Humanistic Psychology*. New York: McGraw-Hill, 1967.

Button, Alan D. "The Psychodynamics of Alcoholism: An Empirically Based Schema," *Quarterly Journal of Studies on Alcohol*, Vol. XVII, No. 4 (Yale University Press, 1956).

Erikson, Erik H. *Identity: Youth and Crisis*, New York: W. W. Norton and Co., 1968.

Evans, Richard I. "Dialogue with Erik Erikson," *Psychiatry and Social Science Review*, Vol. I, No. 4 (1967), p. 12.

BIBLIOGRAPHY

Flavell, John H. *The Developmental Psychology of Jean Piaget*. Princeton: Van Nostrand Co., Inc., 1963.

Freud, Anna. "Adolescence," *The Psychoanalytic Study of the Child*, Vol. XIII, 1958.

Heidegger, Martin. *Being and Time*. New York: Harper and Row, 1963.

Jackson, Donald. "Mike Bell Is Waiting," *Life*, June 7, 1968.

Kierkegaard, Sören. *The Concept of Dread*. Princeton: Princeton University Press, 1944.

Kohlbert, Lawrence. "Development of Moral Character and Ideology," *Review of Child Development Research* (N. L. Hoffman, ed.), Russell Sage, 1964

Kohlbert, Lawrence. "The Child as a Moral Philosopher," *Psychology Today*, Vol. 2, No. 4 (September, 1968).

Kounin, Jacob S., and Gump, Paul V. "The Comparative Influence of Punitive and Nonpunitive Teachers upon Children's Concepts of School Misconduct," *Journal of Educational Psychology*, 1961, LII, 44–49.

May, Rollo (ed.). *Existential Psychology*. New York: Random House, 1967.

Piaget, Jean. *The Moral Judgment of the Child*. New York: MacMillan Co., 1955.

Piaget, Jean. *Six Psychological Studies*. New York: Random House, 1967.

Schutz, William C. *Joy: Expanding Human Awareness*. New York: Grove Press, 1967.

Shostrom, Everett. *Man, the Manipulator*. Nashville: Abingdon Press, 1967.

Watson, Goodwin. "What Do We Know About Learning?" *National Education Association Journal*, March, 1963.

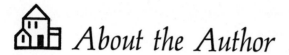 *About the Author*

Alan DeWitt Button was born and grew up in Hood River, Oregon. He was graduated from the University of Oregon and received his Ph.D. in Clinical Psychology from Stanford University in 1953.

At present Dr. Button is a Professor of Psychology at Fresno State College, California, and has a private practice in clinical psychology. He lives in Fresno with his wife and their three children.